DRIVEN BY THE HEART

A Guide to Passionate Living

TONY POLLARD

New York | Los Angeles | London | Sydney

ISBN: 978-1-952884-93-1

WHAT OTHERS ARE SAYING

"Do you want to be inspired? Read one or twenty chapters in Tony's book, "From the Heart." You will be motivated, inspired and encouraged. You will be able to share the heartfelt stories with your team, your children and your audience to inspire them too. This is a book you won't want to put down and I guarantee that you'll be picking it up repeatedly."

- Deborah S Reisdorph, *Esq., author, speaker, attorney*
Founder, BARE Bully Awareness Resistance Education, Inc.

"Engaging. Fun and educational at the same time."

- SSGT FULLWOOD

"We recently had Tony speak at our first annual employee training. Not only was he well received by our employees he was easy to work with, personable and spent extra time with our employees and the other speakers. His high energy and enthusiasm were amazing. You will not be disappointed when hiring Tony for your next event."

- Stacey White, *General Manager, Arab Electric Cooperative, Inc.*

"Tony spoke at a national conference and was very engaging and funny! I would recommend Tony to anyone wanting to motivate a team."

- ALABAMA STATE DIRECTOR OF TRANSPORTATION, ALSDE

"Anthony 'practices what he preaches' and shows that his pragmatic approach can be used by leaders of all levels, when he speaks to groups. The tools and insight he shares in his book have been instrumental in elevating my leadership and results. It's required reading for any leader looking to play to his or her strengths and motivate others. If you want to make your mark as a motivational leader, engage in thoughtful words and act on them, this the book for you."

- Hope Zeanah, *Assistant Superintendent, Baldwin County Public Schools*

"Mr. Pollard has the ability to hold the audience in the palm of his hand. His energy and passion combined with his subject matter knowledge is captivating. In speaking with professional staff members, parents, or students, Mr. Pollard makes clear, concise points that can move audiences to tears and laughter. Mr. Pollard challenges each person to set goals. By using his easy to remember key words or phrases, he makes audiences of all ages leave with a new goal and action steps in mind!"

- Tonya B. Harrelson, Assistant Principal, Fairhope Middle School

"Tony blew it out of the water! We are definitely going to have him back to do more training for us!"

- EXECUTIVE, BALDWIN EMC

"I had the pleasure of working with Tony to help one of our Alabama Rural Electric Cooperatives transition Chief Executive Officers. His genuine realistic presentation style using real life successes and failure to connect to his audience is fantastic. I would highly recommend Tony's presentations to any group looking to build a more effective team."

- Matty Garr Vice-President Statewide Services at AREA-Alabama Rural Electric Association

"Tony has written these stories with such heartfelt words! I have loved all the stories and they have made me better from reading them! Tony has a heart bigger than all the outdoors and desires serve others fully."

- Dr. Connie Jo Williams

"A truly immersive experience!"

- A1C HUFFCUT

"We have brought Tony in to speak to our employees in a big group setting as well as small groups. He is always a hit because he tries to connect to the audience. Employees have left his sessions feeling more energized and ready to approach their jobs with a renewed outlook. One thing he does extremely well is make his speaking engaging. The audience stays focused and can actually apply the things he is teaching in their everyday lives. Tony is a great choice for many different groups."

*- **Melissa Hollingsworth***
Manager of Training and Development, Baldwin EMC

Inspirational. I've began doing things 'from the heart' since then.

- SSGT GANAL

"Tony is an exceptional leader that is dedicated to perfecting his craft. During the time frame I have known Tony, he has been a champion for investing in others, personal growth, and has a razor-sharp focus for excellence. He has a unique skillset as an educator and "Citizen Soldier", which makes him a valuable leader and team member. His individual growth as a leader is nothing short of intentional. He understands the challenges of leadership and truly enjoys serving for the greater good."

*- **Colonial Anthony Sampson**, United States Army Reserves*

"Your presentation was just what I needed, when I needed it. Your words allowed me to put a rough patch behind me and find a renewed joy in my new job. Thank you for using your gifts to enable me to use mine."

- KAREN BARTL, TEACHER

TABLE OF CONTENTS

Introduction 11

Chapter I: Providing Service 15

    Heart of Service 15

    Heart of Comfort 19

    Heart of Self-Sacrifice 24

    Heart of Commitment 29

    Heart of Generosity 33

    Heart of Kindness 37

Chapter 2: Being an Innovator for Change 41

    Heart of Persistence 41

    Heart of Influencer 44

    Heart of Optimism 49

    Heart of Creativity 55

    Heart of Action 58

    Heart of Invention 62

Chapter 3: Pursuing A Purpose 69

    Heart of Gentleness 69

    Heart of Freedom 74

    Heart of Determination 78

    Heart of a Champion 83

    Heart of Courage 87

Chapter 4: Creating Opportunities 95

    Heart of Moxie 95

    Heart of Dreams 100

    Heart of Daring 103

    Heart of a Child 108

    Heart of Joy 113

Chapter 5: Standing Out/ Taking Charge 117

    Heart of Leadership 117

    Heart of Dedication 124

    Heart of Enthusiasm 129

    Heart of Peacemaker 133

    Heart of a Warrior 138

Chapter 6: Embracing Your Choices 143

    Heart of Play 143

    Heart of Loyalty 146

    Heart of Confidence 148

    Heart of Humility 152

    Heart of Honor 155

Chapter 7: Bouncing Back from Adversity 157

    Heart of Resilience 157

    Heart of Devotion 163

    Heart of Stoicism 168

    Heart of Ownership 172

Epilogue 177

INTRODUCTION

What are the things we do from the heart? What drives ordinary people to step up their game and achieve extraordinary things when all hope, desire, and motivation seem lost?

When my daughter was born, my whole heart was devoted to her. I knew from the moment she let out her first cry, that I would be her warrior, protector and guide through life. When I became a single parent, I pledged that my entire being would be devoted to raising her with joy and cheer in my heart.

While serving in Operation Desert Storm in the early 1990s I became extremely close to my friends and teammates. We knew we would protect each other no matter what horrors we would experience when the actual battles began. As our unit maneuvered from one battle to the next we protected one another both physically and mentally. I would have laid my life down for my team and they would have done the same for me.

As schoolteacher, I loved working with my students. Each one held a special place in my heart. They helped me grow as much as I hope I helped them to grow. Had our little school in Alabama been attacked by an active shooter or terrorist, my heart would have been filled with unimaginable emotion. What would I have done? Would I have frozen in the moment or would I have protected the students in my care?

We are capable of amazing things when we do them from the heart. We can accomplish any goal we set when we put our heart into accomplishing that goal. Our experience with that goal becomes singular in focus. Our goal becomes a part of who we are.

When my ex-wife and I first brought my daughter Haley home from the hospital I literally slept on the floor beside her crib for two weeks. My heart belonged to her and I would have done anything to see to her safety, love, and care. As Haley grew and started playing sports, I attended each event with joy and love in my heart.

The things we do from the heart are real and help to shape who we will be in life. The things we do from the heart help determine our worth and our character. My character has been shaped many times over. Each time my heart has been involved or truly devoted to something I have grown from it.

While in the army I had to have a heart of courage, a heart of resilience, discipline, and perseverance. While raising Haley, I had to have a heart of loyalty, care, joy, service, patience, confidence, and play. Each of these "hearts", represent a story or moment that have shaped my life. Each of us have stories within, that shape our lives, that determine our character. We are all works in progress and we can determine to mold ourselves into people of strong character and will. We can accomplish anything if we choose to get up, get moving, and put our heart into the thing we choose to do. The extraordinary thing that you go after may seem crazy to some, but if you do not attempt it, you will not be living from your heart. If you are looking to do more with your life, then you must start to live through your heart.

I discovered many of the stories in this book after a career setback that nearly crushed my spirit. As I sought to learn from the devastating experience and begin my own journey to living a life with my whole heart, I started reading and listening to inspiring stories of people doing extraordinary things. I read or listened to well over 350 books over a five-year period. These people included family, friends, work-colleagues, and people that I researched. We do not learn just by reading about famous people. We learn and grow by listening to our own heart. We learn and grow by listening to our friends and relatives. Wisdom is gained when we take a step back and just watch the world around us. As I read and listened, I assigned each person a word from the heart. In business, we work with diverse populations and recognizing strengths and weaknesses can only make us better. The people in these stories have taken their setbacks, their strengths, their talents, and the drive to do something different, and special to a new level.

The stories I chose resonated with me and touched me profoundly. Each story has helped me in my own journey, to grow as a man seeking to live a full life.

I hope these stories touch you the way that have touched me. These are the stories of women, men, animals, soldiers, inventors, boxers, and many others from a broad diverse group. Create a new you, discover the beating heart and the drive from each individual written about. Be open to change and grow as each story is a testament to what we are capable of when we live through the heart.

CHAPTER 1

PROVIDING SERVICE

Heart of Service
Hazen Pingree

"The best way to find yourself is to lose yourself in the service of others."
- Mahatma Gandhi

I was a military brat growing up. My dad was in the Army, stationed all over the world. We lived in Germany, Colorado, Kentucky, and South Carolina before my dad finally retired from active duty. I had a great childhood while my dad served and I learned a lot about how to treat people from how he took care of his soldiers.

My dad was not around a lot as his military obligations kept him doing training or traveling. When he was home, however, he would often have soldiers over at our house, particularly those who weren't married or didn't have family nearby. If you have served, then you know being a single soldier is not easy, particularly a young, enlisted soldier. You're away from your family for an extended period, plus you don't make a lot of money. My dad often brought soldiers over on the weekends to stay with us, eat with us, and be a part of our family. My dad loved to serve his soldiers and make them a part of our lives as much as possible.

I remember one Thanksgiving morning I was riding with my dad to the commissary, or military grocery store, to get some rolls. My dad saw a soldier walking alone on the base and pulled over and invited him to our house for the holiday meal. The soldier's eyes lit up and he got in the truck with us and enjoyed a holiday meal, no strings attached. I have always admired my dad for his generosity and the thoughtful service he has always provided to as many people as he can.

When I was a teacher, my dad and I would adopt a needy family from my class and make sure they had a nice Christmas. My student and their family had no idea where the Christmas gifts and food came from as we adopted them through the school counselor or administrator. We did this to provide service to a family in need without seeking any credit for ourselves. Providing service is simple and it does not have to involve money. It can just be a kind gesture.

My fleet manager, Glenn Brown, and I taught a class on providing service to our department heads. We wanted to remind our employees that we do more than repair and provide school buses for our school district. We reminded them that one kind act can change the trajectory of someone's day, month, or life. It is up to all of us to provide service to others.

Hazen Pingree was a member of the wealthy elite in Detroit Michigan, who found his calling providing service to his community in a way he never expected.

After serving in the Union army during the Civil War, he found his way to Detroit in 1866. He teamed up with Charles Smith and started a very successful shoe company. By the 1890's their shoe company became the largest manufacturer of shoes in the American West. As his company prospered, he became part of the wealthy establishment of Detroit and many of his peers pressed him to run for mayor. Ping, as he became known, would tell them he was too busy making shoes to run for political office. In fact, he thought they were crazy for approaching him with such a preposterous idea.

Eventually his peers in the Republican party wore him down and he successfully ran for mayor in 1890. Once in office, Ping, being a political novice, soon realized that the city of Detroit was being run by crooked politicians. This inspired him to press for reforms at all levels. With a mean temper and boundless energy, he fought corruption and special interests. Ping fought on behalf of the poor, working class even though he was among Detroit's elite.

He got private corporations to lower the price of natural gas, telephone service and street car rates. The citizens of Detroit were paying double or more of what other large cities were paying. Ping reconstructed the sewers and improved roads that were considered among the worst in the United States. He exposed corruption in the school board and bribery within the private lighting company. Ping threw himself into the job of mayor and worked to changed Detroit at all levels.

When Ping became mayor, he promoted progressive reforms throughout Detroit on behalf of all its citizens, not just the well-connected. He attacked the problems of the city like a mother bear protecting her cubs.

In 1893, the city and the country were gripped by a depression. The poor citizens of Detroit were on the verge of starvation as there were no shelters and systems in place to care for families without jobs and incomes. Ping reached out to his wealthy friends for help and many turned him down while commenting that the poor were just lazy and did not want to work. The situation was becoming desperate for some people as the depression wore on.

Ping and his wife cared deeply for the citizens and the Detroit itself but didn't know how to help. After riding together through the city streets one weekend, his wife had an idea. She suggested using the empty city lots to plant food for those who needed it.

Ping loved the idea and he again reached out to churches and the wealthy for help with little success. He only raised around 14 dollars from his efforts. Undaunted, he put up his prized thoroughbred horse for auction to help raise the money needed for the project. He eventually raised enough money to buy gardening tools, implements, and seed. He got the owners of the empty lots to donate the land and set up applications for those willing to work in the gardens. The city was flooded with applications from those citizens that were called lazy by the wealthy.

Ping even brought in an officer from the U.S. Cavalry, fittingly named Captain Cornelius Gardener, to oversee and help train the workers on proper gardening techniques. Soon enough, gardens of potatoes and vegetables were springing up all over Detroit. The gardens yielded enough food to help the citizens survive the harsh winter and Ping earned the new nickname the "Potato Patch King." In a time of need, he demonstrated a true heart of service toward his city and the community.

Hazen Pingree would go onto to serve four terms as mayor of Detroit and was still in office when he was elected governor of Michigan. Ping was so devoted to Detroit he wanted to continue as mayor, while serving as governor. This was challenged in the courts and Ping had to make a choice. He went on to serve as governor of Michigan for two terms.

Ping found the challenges of corruption and change were much harder at the state level but he persevered for those two terms nonetheless. In the book, "The American Mayor" published in 1999, he is identified by the U.S. scholars as one of the top 10 mayors in U.S. history. He led the city out of the 19th century and into the 20th century with his ideas and progressive changes. Pingree was not only a great leader but his service to others stands out as a testament to his courage, compassion, and fighting spirit to help those in need.

My dad has been a fine example of helping and providing service to others. He would invite strangers into our home and care for them as if they were family. Hazen Pingree inspired an entire city to work together for the good of all. Though one of the first public works projects in the country, he was able to help those he served during their darkest hours. Live life with a heart of service.

Questions:

1. Do you feel like it's important to serve others? Why or why not?
2. You don't have to be an elected official to serve and your acts can be large or small. How do you serve others?
3. What lesson did you learn from your parents that shaped your values today?

Heart of Comfort
Janusz Korczak

"Sometimes the best way to help someone is just to be near them."
- Veronica Roth

When Haley was eight years old she woke up with a terrible fever and a temperature hovering around 102 degrees. I called in to work and took off for the day to take her to the doctor. The doctor diagnosed her with strep-throat prescribed her some medication and sent her home to rest for a couple of days. I went to the grocery store and got her some soup, comfort food, and juice, and picked up a couple of movies from the video store, two words you don't hear much anymore.

When we got home she changed into some comfortable clothes. We put a movie in and she laid her head in my lap and quickly fell asleep. I rubbed her head and before I knew it I fell asleep myself. We were both suddenly awakened when Haley started gagging. She threw up all over me and, having a weak stomach, I immediately threw up as well.

Vomit was everywhere! I got Haley and myself cleaned up as quick as I could before I threw up again. Once the excitement was over, Haley and I comforted one other and even laughed about the situation. Years later, Haley and I still laugh about that day. More than anything we are reminded that we provided comfort for each other and we took care of each other from the heart.

As a father, my job was to provide comfort and love when needed. When our family, friends, or colleagues are in pain or are suffering, we should take the time to provide them with comfort. To console them in their time of need.

When I first started teaching, my principal, Connie Jo, provided me with comfort when I needed it the most. I was a non-tenured, first-year teacher in the school district. But my personal life was in turmoil. My wife had left me and I was in the middle of a divorce. I also had custody of Haley. I was nervous sharing this personal information with Connie Jo but I knew it might affect me and my focus as a teacher and I wanted her to know what was going on.

Connie Jo could have used this information as an excuse to get rid of me. Instead, she looked at me from behind her desk, got up and hugged me. Then she said, "We are going to get through this together." I will never forget those words and how much they meant to me in that moment. Connie Jo, who hardly knew me, made a promise to help me get through my divorce. She demonstrated a true heart of comfort in one of the most trying times of my life.

Providing comfort isn't always easy, but you must do it from the heart above all else. Henryk Goldszmit, who was better known by his pseudonym Janusz Korczak, provided comfort in the most dire situations. Janusz was a Polish children's author, pediatrician, and child advocate who designed systems and programs for children.

At an early age, he was forced to work to take care of his family after his father had died, while attending school to become a pediatrician. He served as a doctor during the Russo/Japanese war in the early 1900's. During this time, his devotion to children grew. He once bought a stick from a Chinese teacher who was using it to beat children just to keep them from being abused. The stick was later used by the children to jump rope with. Janusz studied practices from orphanages in Britain and Berlin and developed his own style which contrasted with the many harsh Polish orphanages of the day.

Janusz submitted his literary work for children and began to get published. His children's books were popular and in later years German soldiers offered to help him escape from the Warsaw Ghetto because his books were so beloved by their own children.

Janusz became director of Dom Seirot in 1911, an orphanage he designed for Jewish children in Warsaw. Using his tremendous insight into the hearts and minds of children, he developed and created a new way of running orphanages. He encouraged dialogue with children, empowered them to participate in their own care and designed systems that promoted democratic participation by the children. These programs were extremely novel for the day.

The Germans attacked Poland in 1939. Janusz volunteered for the Polish Army but, at 61, he was considered too old to serve. The Germans quickly routed Poland and within a month the country surrendered to the Germans. By 1940 the Germans established the Warsaw ghetto, a place for Jews to be housed until they could be transported to the concentration camps. Those that lived in the small confines of the ghetto were given meager rations, as little as 150 calories a day. This amounts to a small bag of peanuts or a Coke.

At the time, Janusz served as director for two orphanages; one which housed Catholic children and the other Jewish children. After the establishment of the Ghetto, German soldiers paid a visit and informed him the Jewish orphanage would have to move there, but he could continue to serve as the director of the Catholic orphanage. Janusz refused the offer and chose to go into the Ghetto, along with 12 staff members and 196 Jewish children.

Starvation, typhus, and many other diseases were rampant in the ghetto. Janusz again was offered sanctuary. In addition to the offer from the German soldiers, a Red Cross delegation tasked with checking for human rights violations offered to get Janusz out of the Ghetto. But he refused to leave the children to whom he provided care and comfort and spurned the offer, which would have provided his escape from the terrible conditions of the ghetto and an uncertain future.

Janusz, his staff and the children would endure this burden together. The adults did their best to provide comfort to the children, giving up their rations and making sure they had clean clothing. They would sing songs and help the children continue their education as best they could. Janusz and his staff tried to provide as much comfort and normalcy as possible for the two years they lived in the ghetto, as conditions worsened and atrocities grew.

In 1942, the Germans came to Janusz and told him to prepare the orphans to be shipped off in the trains. While the German soldiers often told those in the Ghetto they were being transported to safer place with better housing and a higher level of subsistence, Janusz knew better. He knew their destination was most likely the extermination camp known as Treblinka. Unlike concentration camps, these camps had one sole purpose, to kill those sent there.

Knowing Janusz's life was in peril, a friend and colleague entered the ghetto with papers that would have allowed his release. Janusz was incensed by the suggestion that he abandon the children and berated his friend and sent him on his way.

On the day of their departure, Janusz gathered his staff and made sure the children were prepared to go to the extermination camp. He had the children dress in their best clothes and each carried a blue knapsack and their favorite toy on their way to the deportation point. He told the orphans they were going out into the country, so they ought to be cheerful. At last they would be able to exchange the horrible suffocating city walls for meadows of flowers, streams where they could bathe, woods full of berries and mushrooms.

They came out into the yard, two by two, nicely dressed and in a happy mood. Survivors of the Ghetto tell stories of the orphans marching through the ghetto to the trains singing and joyously holding hands. As they arrived at the trains to be deported, legend has it that an SS soldier recognized Janusz and offered to help him escape. He gently refused and stated that he must provide his children with comfort until the end. The children, staff and Janusz boarded the trains never to be heard from again.

Janusz lived and died providing a heart of comfort. Though he had many opportunities to save his own life, he instead sacrificed his life for those in his care. His sacrifice and life are celebrated in Jewish lore.

My principal provided the comfort I needed at a time of great personal distress. I was worried about losing my job and not being strong enough to take care of Haley. Connie Jo, or Boss Lady as I later called her, gave me a simple hug and some encouraging words. Her act of comfort gave me peace when I needed most.

Questions:

1. When was the last time you provided comfort to someone in need?
2. Janusz was a leader. Do you feel having a heart of comfort is necessary to be a good leader?
3. If you were in Janusz's shoes, would have taken one of his many opportunities to escape? Why or why not?

Heart of Self-Sacrifice
Irena Sendler

"Love is willing self-sacrifice for the good of another that does not require reciprocation or that the person being loved is deserving."
- Paul David Tripp

When I was a child, my dad would not touch his plate of food until he knew my brother and I had eaten. This little act of eating last was his demonstration of self-sacrifice in our family. My mother did the same. We did not have a lot growing up, but she made sure my brother and I wore clothes that were not tattered or falling apart, even if she had to wear clothes that were.

When I joined the Army, and was promoted to sergeant, I made sure my soldiers were taken care of before me. As a father and leader, it is important to me to make sure the well-being of my daughter, wife, and those that work for me comes before my own. I want them to know I am willing to sacrifice so they do not have to.

While serving in Desert Storm, I would have sacrificed my life for my teammates. As soldiers, we are trained to take care of the buddy next to you and those you serve with. It is taught from the moment you join the military that you put the team first. One day, while training before the ground war started, a torrential rain hit. We were in the middle of one of driest deserts in the world and it started raining out of nowhere. It rained so fast and hard that the foxhole we had just completed two days prior filled up with water. All our gear and clothing were soaked and any clothing we had laid out was as well.

Once the rain stopped, I was one of the only guys that had any dry clothing as I had just put some items in a wet weather bag. I shared what I had with my teammates and we laid our wet clothing out to dry. We often sacrificed for each other and did so with a willing heart. It has been nearly 30 years since Desert Storm and those I served with are still some of the best friends I have ever had. We share a bond that many cannot and hopefully will never have to comprehend. Ours was a heart of sacrifice in all types of weather, environments and war.

One of my friends, Felix, was willing to sacrifice himself to save others whose vehicle had been hit by friendly fire. With no regard for himself and in the blazing flames, he opened the hatch to access those trapped inside the Bradley fighting vehicle, a light armored troop carrier, and began pulling his teammates out of the vehicle. During this heroic act, Felix was exposed to depleted uranium.

Felix demonstrated the willingness to sacrifice himself in the face of danger. Little did he know at the time, but his bravery that day would catch up with him years later. Felix died of a brain tumor ten years after the war. Doctors suspected the cause of the tumor was his exposure to chemicals and the depleted uranium that one fateful night. Felix demonstrated a true heart of self-sacrifice and paid the ultimate price.

In September 1939, the German Army invaded Poland with ferocity. The Polish Army surrendered in just over a month of conflict. The Germans then established the Warsaw Ghetto in the fall of 1940 to contain the Jews. A ten-foot high wall was built around the ghetto and guards were posted all along the wall so the Jewish people could not travel in or out. At its peak, the ghetto housed nearly 500,000 Jews in an area of just over a mile. Some estimates state that each room available in the Ghetto housed nine Jewish people. Can you imagine being stuffed in small rooms with nine other people? The Germans provided meager rations for those housed in the ghetto and did not care if the people starved to death. This was all part of the "Final Solution," the German plan for the genocide of all Jews.

The health of the Jews in the Ghetto began to deteriorate. Families were being torn apart as more and more Jews were sent to concentration camps. Jews were sent to horrific camps such as Treblinka, where over 900,000 of them were put to death. As the Ghetto grew, so did starvation, malnutrition, diseases from a lack of health care, and many more atrocities. Over 92,000 Jews died in the Ghetto of starvation and sickness alone.

Polish citizens were not blind to all the pain and suffering that the Jews were experiencing. Many brave people were willing to help the Jewish people. One of these brave people was Irena Sendler.

Irena was a social worker who had credentials to enter the ghetto in order to check for the spread of diseases which could also affect the German soldiers. Irena witnessed the starvation and the sickness of the Jewish people firsthand and felt compelled to save the children. With the help of a resistance group, Irena devised a plan to rescue as many children as she could. Irena had one problem, though, how to convince Jewish mothers and parents into letting her and her group take their children. As a father, I would not have given up my daughter when she was young.

Irena possessed a gentle voice and a kind heart, but she spoke the unvarnished truth. She explained to the Jewish parents that while she could not guarantee the safety of their children if they allowed her to take them, the odds were better than if they stayed in the ghetto where they would surely die or be sent to the concentration camps. What a choice! I can only imagine the turmoil this caused for these parents, knowing that what was probably best for their children meant they may never see them again. For the children, it must have been terrifying to be forced to go with strangers. As for Irena and the members of the resistance, they were jeopardizing their lives to get the children safely out of the Ghetto.

Irena and the resistance devised many ingenious ways to evacuate the children. If they were infants, they were sedated and put at the bottom of toolboxes. Other children were smuggled out of the city through the sewer pipes. Older children were told to fake being extremely ill and Irena would tell the German soldiers that they were contagious and needed to be evacuated or risk spreading a disease that could affect them as well.

Irena and her group would sedate nervous children and tell the Germans they had died and the bodies needed to be buried. Once outside the Ghetto, children were placed with families until after the war in a hope of reuniting the parents with their children. In all Irena and her resistance group saved over 2500 children during the war. Irena had a heart of self-sacrifice, yet she knew her own life would be sacrificed if she was caught by the German Army.

In an act of defiance, Irena would put the children's names, addresses, and parent's information in jars and bury them under an old apple tree outside the German barracks. I like to imagine she did this in the middle of the night and then would smile at the barracks that housed the German soldiers. Irena was small and petite, yet brave.

Irena's luck ran out on October 18, 1943 when the Gestapo arrested her. She was taken into custody and interrogated. Though she was beaten and tortured daily, she never gave up any of the locations of the children. Her true heart of sacrifice was put to the test. One of her legs and feet were broken. The Gestapo probably tried to entice her to reveal information with medication to ease the pain. After days of torture, Irena was sentenced to death. Still, she held her tongue and was willing to sacrifice her own life to protect the children and those who had sheltered them during the war.

A last-minute bribe to a German soldier saved Irena's life as she was on her way to the firing squad. She was set free and would spend the final years of the war in hiding.

After the war, Irena tried to reunite the children with their parents. Sadly, many of them had died in the concentration camps. The children were adopted by those who had taken them in during the war. Many others were taken in by other families and some were reunited with their parents.

In the years after the war, Irena never sought attention for her deeds and lived a happy, quiet life in Soviet-occupied Poland. In her later years, Irena was finally recognized for her bravery and sacrifice to save the children of the Ghetto. In true Irena fashion, she was humbled by the accolades and only wished she could have done more. Irena looked at the children she saved as her own. Though Irena experienced great pain and torture, she put others needs above her own and lived with a heart of self-sacrifice.

My friend, Felix, charged into a dangerous situation to save fellow soldiers and ultimately sacrificed his life for his actions. Irena Sendler put the needs of 2500 children ahead of her own well-being and was nearly executed for her deeds. But you don't have to risk your life to live with a heart of self-sacrifice. That can be demonstrated in acts both big and small or as simple as my father waiting until my brother and I were full to take his first bite of dinner.

Questions:

1. What was your latest act of self-sacrifice?
2. Do find acts of self-sacrifice like Irene Sendler's foolish or admirable? Why?
3. Do you feel like a heart of self-sacrifice is important? Why or why not?

Heart of Commitment
Shania Twain

The quality of a person's life is in direct proportion to their commitment to excellence, regardless of their chosen field of endeavor.
- Vince Lombardi

I learned many lessons serving in the military. One of the most important was commitment to our team and the mission. From the moment you arrive at boot camp, you are put in situations which force you to work as a team and be committed to one another. This commitment was put to the test many times during my four years of active duty stationed in Germany and serving in Desert Storm.

In Germany, our training missions were geared toward commitment and teamwork. On one training mission, my friends John, Mike and I were tasked with marching 20 miles with full battle gear in a set amount of time. We were given a map with coordinates to locate and had to conquer impediments along the way. For example, a course director might say that John had been shot and Mike and I had to care for him or that we could only use hand signals to communicate while navigating a situation.

We loved this type of training. It was fun and it brought us closer together as friends and teammates. We were committed to the mission but we were more committed to one another. If one of us lagged behind, the other two would carry his gear. If one of us began to have negative thoughts, the other two would preach positive affirmations. At one point, I remember whistling the tune, "American Pie" by Don McLean to lift our spirits. This song helped us to overcome our challenges and achieve our ultimate mission. It took us several hours to complete the 20 miles, but we did do it within the allotted time frame.

The three of us are still friends to this day. Our military training taught us much more than how to be soldiers. It taught us commitment to a cause and to your battle buddy. It taught us to care about more than ourselves.

When my daughter was born, I knew exactly where my commitment would lie. It would be toward Haley and I would be her protector as much as her father.

Our children have a profound effect on our hearts. While my commitment to my Army teams was strong, my bond and commitment to Haley were naturally even stronger. We are willing to do anything for our children. When our heart is involved we can take our level of commitment to stratospheric places.

One famous singer's heart of commitment was challenged from the very beginning. Born Eileen Regina Edwards, Shania Twain overcame a difficult upbringing to rise to the top of the pop and country charts.

Shania' parents divorced when she was young. Her mother Sharon soon met Jerry Twain, a member of the Ojibwe Native American Tribe in Canada. Jerry and Sharon struggled financially and the family lived in extreme poverty. Later in life, Shania told stories of eating sandwiches with a filling of only mayonnaise or mustard. On top of the struggles the family endured financially, Jerry was an abusive alcoholic. He would often beat Sharon physically and berate her. Shania and her siblings often witnessed this abuse by their father. They became committed to one another as a result of the trauma they experienced together.

Shania's musical talents were recognized at an early age by her mother Sharon. Shania began singing at three and was playing guitar by eight. By the age of 10, she was writing her own songs.

Sharon took any extra money the family could scrounge up and invested it in furthering Shania's musical talents, in music and singing lessons. As a child, Shania began to play in clubs and at events. She was also featured on Canadian television. Shania became committed to building her musical career.

Shania's talents started to pay off and the family used her earnings to survive. Though the family wasn't struggling as much, the abuse by Jerry continued. He once strangled Sharon so hard and for so long her body went limp. Shania would often intervene in these confrontations and would pay for it with physical, verbal and even sexual abuse. Through it all Shania remained committed to her calling and her family.

When Shania turned 18, her heart of commitment to her music led her from her small town of Timmins, Ontario to Toronto and later to Nashville. As she struggled to get her career started, she supplemented her singing income by working at McDonalds. As her career started to get some traction, tragedy struck. In 1987, Sharon and Jerry were killed in an automobile accident. Shania had to move back home to care for her four siblings.

Shania was only 23 when she took on the role of full-time mother. She took a job singing at a Vegas style show at resort in Ontario to help support the family. Ever committed to her dreams of singing and writing songs, she worked day and night to fulfill her dreams and care for her brother and sisters. While I am sure she had moments where she wanted to give up, she stayed committed.

Once her siblings were on their own, she assembled and distributed a demo, which caught the attention of Mercury Nashville Records. The company signed her to a contract with one condition. The record execs did not like her first name Eileen, so she changed it to Shania, which means "on my way," in Ojibwe. Shania's heart of commitment to herself and her family helped her to be successful.

Shania became a superstar in the 1990s as her country songs successfully crossed over into pop music as well. She became a top star in both genres. She has sold millions of copies of her albums and won numerous awards, including five Grammys.

Her life has not been without setbacks, however. She went through a bitter divorce from her first husband, Mutt Lange, who produced several of her most successful albums. She developed dysphonia, which is a tightening of the vocal muscles, which affected her voice and sidelined her career for years. Shania remained committed and released new music and has become one of the most successful female artists of all times.

Inspired by her own upbringing, Shania started a foundation, Shania Kids Can Foundation, to help underprivileged children whose lives are negatively affected by domestic abuse and poverty. She has pledged to help support children who have had to suffer like she and her siblings did.

Shania's life should shine as an example of what we are capable of when we have a heart of commitment. But you don't have to be a superstar to fully live your commitment. In the Army, I was committed to my teammates and comrades. As a father, I have been and will continue to be committed to my daughter. Shania was committed to her siblings and to her music, a heart of commitment that never failed through poverty, abuse, success and setbacks. Where is your heart of commitment?

Questions:

1. To whom or what are you most committed?
2. What experience did you have that taught you to care more about yourself than others?
3. Who has a heart of commitment that you admire?

Heart of Generosity
Chuck Feeney

"When you stop giving and offering something to the
rest of the world, it's time to turn out the lights."
- George Burns

I was speaking to my friend, Vinny, this morning and he shared a story about his youngest daughter, Hope. She wanted to borrow some money so she could wear pajamas to school. She explained that the money was going to a boy in her school who had cancer.

My friend saw an opportunity to teach Hope about giving. He told her how proud he was of her wanting to give money to help her friend battle cancer. He added that her piggy bank still had a few dollars in it, which should be enough.

Hope gave him a weird look and asked why he wasn't giving her the money. He explained this was her cause and she needed to use her own money. He had his own causes and this was not one he wanted to add to his list. Hope, pulling the oldest kid trick in the book, said she would ask her mom for the money.

Vinny responded that giving his or her mother's money to help her classmate would not be a contribution from her but a contribution from them. Neither of them would be going to school in pajamas. It wasn't the money that mattered as he and her mother could afford to give. It was how good Hope would feel if she willingly used her own money to support her classmate, which would make being able to wear pajamas to school more rewarding for her.

Hope finally understood her father's point and took the money from her piggy bank. It contained five one-dollar bills, which she gave to her friend.

Hope got to wear pajamas to school because she was willing to give of her own free will. But she also got to experience pride in that she was one of the only kids who contributed their own money and a sense of joy from helping her classmate.

What are you willing to give to help another person? Are you willing to give it all away? If you only had $100, would you give away $99? Philanthropists like Bill and Melinda Gates have set up the Gates Foundation to give away billions to fight poverty and starvation throughout the world. They have pledged to give away their fortune before they die, though they are still far from poor. In 2020, Bill Gates was the second wealthiest man in the world.

Warren Buffett, who is the fourth richest person in the world, has pledged to donate over 99% of his fortune to charity. But 1% of 67.5 billion dollars is still a lot of money to live on.

Chuck Feeney is a man you've probably never heard of, but he inspired both Buffett and Gates. In fact, Buffett once said, "Chuck has set an example."

Feeney was once a wealthy man who pledged to give his money years ago. When he decided to give his fortune away in the 1980s, he was worth well over eight billion dollars. His story epitomizes the heart of generosity and giving.

Charles Francis Feeney was born during the Depression into a working-class Irish-American family in New Jersey. He shoveled snow and sold Christmas cards door-to-door to make money as a child. His family was of modest means, but his parents were charitable and these lessons made an impression on young Chuck.

After serving four years in the U.S. Air Force, where he was stationed in Japan, Chuck went to college on the G.I. Bill. He supported himself by selling sandwiches while he attended Cornell University. Upon graduation he and a college friend Robert Miller, started Duty Free Shops (DFS) shops in the late 1950's selling duty-free import goods to American soldiers.

Being familiar with Japan, Chuck recognized and benefited from its economic boom and saw an opportunity to expand DFS. In 1964, Japan lifted foreign travel restrictions enacted after World War II and Japanese tourists surged across the globe. Chuck hired analysts to predict which cities they would visit and DFS set up locations in popular destinations that included Hawaii, Hong Kong, San Francisco, and even Alaska. They would mark up their goods such as alcohol, cigarettes, and perfume. The pair even hired Asian-speaking guides to lead the tourist to their shops and Japanese sales clerks. DFS boomed and Chuck and Robert brought in a couple of other investors to help them manage the growing business.

Chuck loved making money mostly because he was competitive, but he did not like the trappings of money and this is when he decided to give it all away. In 1984, Chuck started his mission of giving while living. Unbeknownst to his partners, he transferred his 38.75% stake in DFS ownership to Atlantic Philanthropies. His goal was to give away his 8-billion-dollar fortune. He even told close family members he hoped his last checked bounced. Chuck did not just give away his money, he got others to help contribute as well. He even got governments to match funds. His business acumen paid big dividends in increasing the value of his fortune.

For nearly 15 years, he gave away millions without anyone knowing it. The beneficiaries of his generosity were often sworn to secrecy as he did not want to draw attention to himself. Chuck continued to travel the world working for DFS and growing the business, even though he was no longer making any personal gain. It was numerous charities that would benefit.

While traveling to Vietnam, Chuck identified a need for better hospitals and education. Over the years, Atlantic Philanthropies donated $381.5 million to improve public health and revitalize libraries and universities. He gave nearly 937 million to Cornell over his 30 plus years of giving away his fortune. Chuck gave 370 million in grants worldwide for cancer research and education.

As an Irish-American, Chuck was inspired to give 170 million to the University of Limerick in Ireland. In 2001, the Atlantic Fund gave medical grants to Australia's Queensland University of Technology totaling 320 million. The list of his generous gifts goes on and on. Yet none of the buildings or research programs his donations have created bear his name. He never wanted to bring attention to himself. He only desired to give his fortune away to good causes. It was not until 1997 when he sold his stake in DFS that he came public with his philanthropy.

Chuck Feeney has truly lived a life with a heart of giving. It is estimated that by the time he has given his entire fortune away it will have been well over 8.5 billion dollars in gifts to charities, countries, and universities. In 2020 the Atlantic Philanthropies will close its door permanently meaning Chuck Feeney will have fulfilled his goal. At the same time, he has inspired others like Warren Buffet and Bill Gates..

Chuck learned from his parents that it is better to give than receive. Maybe Hope has learned the same lesson from her small charitable act. While we don't have to be like Chuck Feeney and give away our life savings, when we live with a heart of giving and true generosity, we truly do receive much more in return.

Questions:

1. How important do you think it is to be philanthropic?
2. If you were to come into a financial windfall, how would you spend it?
3. What do you think about Chuck Feeney's generosity? Is he crazy? Inspirational?

Heart of Kindness
James Harrison

A tree is known by its fruit; a man by his deeds. A good deed is never lost; he who sows courtesy reaps friendship, and he who plants kindness gathers love.
- Saint Basil

At the end of my ninth grade year my parents divorced, and we had to sell my family home. I was a lost soul. I started partying and drinking and was headed down a path that was not going to be good for me. My grades started falling and I felt trapped and rootless in my changing world.

That changed when I joined the football team. One day, one of my coaches, Coach Leveritt, noticed me sitting off by myself. He came up and started talking to me and asked me how I was doing and seemed genuinely interested. This small act of kindness and subsequent conversations helped me to see my true potential and to feel some direction again. Coach Leveritt demonstrated kindness in what may have been one of my darkest hours.

Teachers exude kindness and demonstrate it daily to students in need. In fact, Coach Leveritt's act of kindness was part of what inspired me to be an educator. These people change the world one student at a time. But how many get to change an entire country because of their kindness?

That is the story of James Harrison. His kindness has saved more than 2.4 million Australian babies. His story is nothing short of miraculous. When James was just 14 he had major chest surgery and over 13 liters of blood were required to save his life. After his surgery, he was in the hospital for three months. During this time, James made the pledge to start donating blood as soon as he was of legal age.

James started donating in 1954. After a few donations, it was discovered that his blood contained extremely rare antibodies, which could be used to fight Rhesus disease in newborns. Rhesus disease is a condition where antibodies in a pregnant woman›s blood destroy her baby›s blood cells. While the condition is not harmful to the mother, it can cause the baby to become anemic and develop jaundice.

James' antibodies were so rare that once doctors discovered out about his life-saving blood his body was insured for over a million dollars. His extraordinary blood was used to make a life-saving medication known as Anti-D. Every batch is created from James's blood. This medication is given to mothers to prevent Rhesus Disease. Even his own daughter received the medication during her pregnancy to ensure his granddaughter was born healthy.

Before the development of Anti-D, thousands of babies died each year, many women had miscarriages, and babies were born with brain damage.

But since 1967 millions of doses of the Anti-D have been prescribed to pregnant mothers and it is estimated that James' blood has helped 2.4 million babies.

None of these extraordinary things are what make James so kind. What makes James so kind is that he did not just donate once. He donated blood or plasma for sixty years despite having a fear of needles. James had to avert his eyes and ignore the pain with each donation.

No wonder he became known as the Man with the Golden Arm. Imagine taking the time to donate so often. Imagine the needle marks that may or may not have healed properly between donations. James truly had a heart of kindness. He was a national hero and has been given many awards throughout his life. He was even given the Medal of the Order of Australia, one of the country's most prestigious honors.

James had to retire from giving blood at the age of 81 for health reasons. But he has left a legacy of changing Australia because of his extreme generosity and kindness that was born from a life-changing moment after his own surgery at 14.

I may not be able to save a country, but as an educator, I can apply the lessons I learned from Coach Leveritt – to help one child at a time with a small act of kindness.

Questions:

1. Have you ever done that something that caused you discomfort because it was the right thing to do? What was it?
2. Is there some small act of kindness you can perform today?
3. Was there ever an instance in your life where a small act of kindness made an enormous difference?

CHAPTER 2

BEING AN INNOVATOR FOR CHANGE

Heart of Persistence
Dashrath Manjhi

"Persistence is to the character of man as carbon is to steel."
Napoleon Hill

My goal is to run a marathon this year so when I woke up this morning, I went for a run. Running twenty-six miles will be daunting and at times I have my doubts if I can do it. The only thing that is driving me is that I want to be able to say I did it.

Millions of people have run a marathon and each person that takes on the challenge must have a heart of persistence. The training can be grueling at times. I did my first half-marathon a few months ago and after running the first six miles, my calves started cramping. Each step I took was excruciating. I remained persistent, though, and completed the race.

Since then, I have had to learn to slow my pace down and adjust how my feet hit the ground. It has paid off. This morning I ran ten miles for the first time without cramping. I had to remain super disciplined with my footwork and monitor each foot strike to prevent cramping. I trudged along persistently slow and disciplined until I reached my destination. It took me two hours, but I didn't cramp.

It will take me being focused, determined, motivated, and persistent in my training to complete the actual marathon. It has taken me months to get in shape and when I take breaks I feel it the next time I run. But I have noticed that persistence pays off. Everything I have ever accomplished has required persistence. If we put our hearts into what we are after and persistently seek the goals we set for ourselves, we can and will have a rich life.

Dashrath Manjhi spent 22 years toiling day and night to carve a path through a mountain so the people of his poor, small village in India could get to the health services they needed. The village was surrounded by the Gehlaur Hills, a low but treacherous mountainous area filled with spiny outcroppings of rock.

Before the path was built, the villagers could go over this dangerous terrain or around it to get to healthcare and schools, a distance of 70 kilometers. After Dashrath built the path, they could get to health services and school by traveling only one kilometer.

Dashrath's story is one of heartbreak, pain, loss, and success. He did not wake up one morning and decide to carve this path. His desire and determination were ignited when his young wife Devi was injured bringing him food as she crossed through the Gehlaur Hills. Dashrath had to carry his wife through the treacherous terrain to get her the care needed. During the trip to the hospital, his wife perished. Dashrath awakened to his mission and began his persistent journey to carve the path his village needed.

But first he had to sell his three goats to pay for a hammer and chisel. Yes, he was going to carve the path using only hand tools. He worked in the fields farming during the day and in the evening using the tools he had purchased he began carving the path.

The people of the village called him a madman. They laughed at him and may have even taunted him. Dashrath persisted though. He learned that heating the rock then pouring cold water on it made it easier to break up. Day and night, he hammered away at the rock and carried it off the treacherous hilltop.

As the years went by and Dashrath slowly began making a path in the hills, the villagers began to admire him and some even gave him food and money to buy tools. Imagine him seeing his wife in his memories as he struck each rock. Imagine the heat he endured in the summer and the cold he endured in the winter. His personal discipline and persistence are awe-inspiring to say the least.

In 1982 Dashrath had completed the path. He began his personal mission in 1960 after his beloved wife had passed. He persisted for the next 22 years toiling away at the rock so that his village would have access to the health care that may have saved her life. The villagers who taunted him and called him Mountain Man must have been elated when the path was completed, that path through the mountain that he carved with only hand tools is 25 feet deep, 30 feet wide and 360 feet long.

Dashrath's heart of persistence did more than create a path for his village; it inspired a nation. He died of cancer in 2007 and is regarded as national hero. His village has access to health care, schools, and services needed to thrive. One of Dashrath's friends started a fund that has helped educate the people of the village to help them slowly move out of extreme poverty. Because the children of the village have access to schools, they now have access to a new life.

Dashrath's heart of persistence led to a life fulfilled.

Questions:

1. What task or issue has required the most persistence from you?
2. Who do you admire most for their persistence?
3. Do you think it takes a little madness to persist at a goal that seems impossible?

Heart of an Influencer
Billie Jean King

"Never underestimate the power of dreams and the influence of the human spirit. We are all the same in this notion: The potential for greatness lives within each of us."
- Wilma Rudolph

When Haley was born, December 15, 1996, I pictured her being successful. It never once crossed my mind that she may have struggles and prejudices because of her sex. I guess as a father, I saw her only her strengths and never thought of potential obstacles.

As she grew, I exposed her to sports and adventures, and encouraged her to face her fears. Her junior year, we took a high school band trip to Universal Studies in Orlando. She was willing to do the Fear Factor game and put this crazy helmet on that was full of bugs. My goal was for her to experience life without self-limits. I wanted to influence her to be willing to change her world without doubt and fear.

When she graduated high school, she joined the National Guard following in my footsteps and started her own adventures. Haley loved all the exciting things she did during basic training and boot camp. She got to challenge herself like she never had before. Army boot camp is designed for recruits to face their fears and insecurities and discover the courageous person within. Haley shot high-powered weapons, went through strenuous obstacle courses, and repelled from towers. Haley faced her fears and was challenged many times.

Now she is 23 and for a while she seemed to have lost her adventurous side. Instead of seeking challenges, she sought comfort, which in her case meant being a small-town waitress. I kept hoping to see her spread her wings again. Then she surprised me and after completing an aeronautics training program, secured a job in this high-paying field. I am a proud father, but I know I only have a small role in her success, the influence I exerted on her when she was younger.

When we spread our wings and face the things that hold us back we not only influence and shape our own future, we may affect the future of others. When I was 17, I joined the Army. When I returned home from my training, two of my friends followed my example and decided to join the military as well. Another friend left our small town life and traveled out of state to go to college. I had unintentionally influenced these people to do something that was uncomfortable for them. That was not my plan at all, I just knew that if I did not join the military I would get stuck in the small town of Robertsdale, Alabama and never experience life for myself or go to college. I was only trying to escape my present situation. Never in my wildest dreams did I think I would influence others.

At 11 years old, Billie Jean King dreamed of changing the world. A natural athlete, who loved softball and basketball, she was encouraged by her parents to find a more ladylike sport.

She was invited by a friend to play tennis at the local country club, a sport she described as one where you could "run, jump, and hit a ball." Those activities happened to be Billie Jean's favorite things to do.

She went home after this one day of tennis and told her parents she wanted a tennis racket. Her dad told her that if she wanted it bad enough she would find a way to pay for it. Her parents expected her and her brother to earn their way in life and did not treat them differently based on their sex. Like her brother, she was expected to find ways to solve her problems and to fight for her beliefs.

Billie Jean noticed the inequality in sports. When she was young, sports were geared toward the boys. Boys could make money playing sports and girls did not have many professional outlets. In tennis, everyone wore white clothes, white shoes, played with white balls and even the players were mostly white and male. In today's tennis landscape, that is hard to imagine as the leading women's tennis player is an African American woman, Serena Williams. And Billie Jean King helped make that landscape possible.

Billie Jean was a natural at tennis. Both of her parents were athletes, her mother a swimmer, her father played basketball and her brother Randy played professional basketball. Billie Jean would practice tennis all day and late into the evenings and at age 14 won her first championship in a southern California tournament. Billie Jean was a powerful tennis player. She could move across the court with ease, had a great backhand, and an extraordinary net game.

Billie Jean began her quest for equality in tennis when she and other professional female players realized the male players were getting paid much more in prize money than the women. In some tournaments, a male champion was awarded four times as much prize money as the female champion received.

In protest, she and a group of eight female tennis stars broke away and formed the Women's Tennis Association. They each signed a contract for one dollar. This was a brave move in the midst of the women's movement. Each of these players would go to town-to-town promoting the new league and would sell their own tickets until they got a sponsor, the Virginia Slims tobacco company and started the Virginia Slims Circuit.

In 1971, Billie Jean became the first female tennis player to earn over $100,000, which was still less than the men received but an improvement. She was the number one ranked female tennis player for six years. In 1972, she won Wimbledon, U.S. Open, and the French Open.

As a tennis star, she won 39 grand slam titles in singles, doubles and mixed doubles, with 20 Wimbledon titles. Billie Jean used her fame, drive, and motivation to influence tennis but in doing so she influenced perceptions of all women.

Billie Jean King may be most famous for the televised spectacle, The Battle of the Sexes exhibition tennis match in September 1973 against Bobby Riggs. Riggs was a 55-year-old former champion who had been a vocal opponent of the women's movement. But he was also a hustler and a showman who recognized a once-in-a-lifetime promotional opportunity. Billie Jean played right along.

He relentlessly taunted Billie Jean before the big match. She, in turn, gave him a squealing piglet, a symbol of male chauvinism. But they were actually friends with one another who just relished the opportunity to cast a spotlight on their respective causes. But once the match started, Billie Jean, recognizing the historical importance of the match, took the match seriously and defeated Bobby Riggs in straight sets 6-4, 6-3, and 6-3.

This was not just a personal win for Billie Jean; it was win for women's sports and the feminist movement. This match was shown live from the Astrodome in Houston Texas and televised to a worldwide audience of 90 million people. It is still one of the most watched tennis matches in history.

While the match was hardly textbook tennis, it helped to change perceptions in both men and women. Billie Jean has fondly told stories of fathers coming up to her after the match and thanking her for giving their daughters something to strive toward.

Billie Jean's influence has gone beyond tennis. Women can now play professional basketball, soccer, and softball. Her influence has far exceeded what she had dreamed of doing at age eleven.

She transcended sports and helped to shape the women's movement. Her goal was to get equal prize money for women in tennis and other sports and while there is not pay equality in all sports, it's much closer.

As an influencer, she challenged the status quo of male domination in tennis while dominating the tennis court. Billie Jean was also passionate and driven about her causes and beliefs, even when they caused her pain and discomfort.

Her influence has been recognized in tennis circles. In 2006, the National Tennis Center, where the U.S. Open tennis tournament is held, was renamed the USTA Billie Jean King National Tennis Center.

I left my small Alabama town for a dream of something bigger for my life. And not only did I attend college, I became an educator. I have served as a teacher and administrator in the public schools for over 22 years, shaping a generation of students.

It is so rewarding to have those kids, many of whom are adults, see me and tell me how much I meant to them. Several of the students I once taught have now become teachers and are influencing this new crop of students. While my sphere of influence will never match what Billie Jean accomplished, our individual actions are powerful and have the potential to change the world. We can all be influencers if just step forward to challenge the status quo.

Questions:

1. Who do you have influence on in your life?
2. What would be some examples of positive and negative influence?
3. Have you ever dreamed of changing the world? What was your dream?

Heart of Optimism
Kris Carr

"How wonderful it is that nobody need wait a single moment before starting to improve the world."
- Anne Frank

In life, we can either be full of negativity or full of optimism. A Harvard Medical School research study of 2300 adults showed that people who are more optimistic have lower blood pressure and better overall health. My next stories are not about the statistics though. They are about living from the heart.

My grandmother, Mary Garretson, was the eternal optimist. I was her first grandchild, so I was the first to call her Granny, which is how I shall refer to her. Granny fully lived with a heart of optimism. But it wasn't always that way.

Granny had a terrible childhood. She was put up for adoption when she was a child. Her adopted parents were migrants who worked the fields in Colorado and New Mexico. The family lived in poverty, but were extremely loving and close knit, which would benefit her greatly in later years.

My grandparents met when they were in their late teens. They married and settled in Golden, Colorado. My grandfather was talented with his hands and helped build the iron tracks that the beer bottles traveled on at the Coors brewery. He had a dark side though; he could not handle his booze. Things were fine for a while but after having four children, his alcoholism turned to physical and emotional abuse.

This abuse was mostly directed at Granny. My mom remembered how she thought my granddad was the best father until he started drinking. Granny more than once ended up at a hospital because of the abuse he inflicted upon her.

One Christmas Eve, my granddad came in drunk, beat my Granny and then destroyed Christmas Tree, the presents, and beat my mom and her siblings. The police were called and my grandfather spent the night in jail. Golden was a small town back then and I am sure the community knew what was taking place in the household. But Granny had nowhere to go and no place to turn, so she endured abuse for several years.

My mom escaped the home by joining the military. Granny was left with two younger children to raise. But by this time, she had reached her limit with my grandfather, so she finally got a divorce.

Though she was free from the abuse of my grandfather, things did not improve for Granny. With two children still at home and no prospects for quality work, they were living in poverty. Granny lost her home because she could not pay the mortgage and then she had a nervous breakdown. My mom and my Aunt Kris, already adults on their own, had her committed to an institution. Their two younger siblings went to live with relatives.

Life could really not have been worse for my Granny. For many years, she had lived an unhappy life but now it had hit a new low. But during the time in the institution, she began to change her outlook.

When Granny was released from the mental institution after 18 months, she made a personal decision to change. Granny first got a job and soon was able to get her two younger children back. She started going to night school to become a nurse. The time in the facility had given her purpose and direction. She wanted to help those who experienced what she had gone through. Rather than being beaten down and discouraged about a life full of adversity, Granny was living a life full of optimism about the future.

Granny graduated and became a registered nurse. She got a job as a mental health nurse in the same facility in which she had been committed. She brought her own home and saved her own money. Granny's new heart of optimism led her to start living fully. She started competing in walking marathons in her sixties. Her new lifestyle and heart of optimism dominated the second half of her life, which was full of joy.

Surprisingly, my grandfather who had been the cause of so much pain when they were young, returned sober and apologetic. They both lived happily together in their later years until his death.

After the death of my grandfather, Granny was diagnosed with cancer. She was in her 80s but you would not have known it. She would send us pictures after having chemotherapy holding up a sign that read, "I am kicking cancer's ass." Her heart of optimism inspired many in her family and her community. Sadly, she passed away from her cancer but she left a legacy. Mary Garretson, Granny, had a true heart of optimism.

We can all decide to be defined by a negative past or present or we can decide to throw out negative thoughts and be positive and optimistic in all we do. Kris Carr decided to do that after receiving terrible news. On Valentine's Day 2003, at the age of 32, Kris was diagnosed with a rare Stage IV incurable cancer called epithelioid hemangioendothelioma in her liver and lungs. But rather than accept her diagnosis, she decided to meet it head on.

Kris decided to change the way she was living. In what she described as her "what the fuck," moment, she attacked her cancer with a brand-new nutritional lifestyle. Her cancer inspired her to not hold anything back and to take complete control of her own well-being. Although the type of cancer she had was slow-growing, there is no cure and Kris is fighting with optimism every day.

"I can still be healthy. I can still feel better, love harder and have a more joyful life." Carr proudly proclaims. With pure optimism, she went on a self-pilgrimage to live a better life. Carr started writing about her experiences and the knowledge she was gaining. Here is this beautiful spirit knowing she is dying but taking in every breath as if it is heavenly and divine. Kris lives life with a heart of optimism.

Kris' journey has led her to not only write best-selling books, she has produced films, including *Crazy Sexy Cancer,* about her journey for self-care. Many thousands of people with cancer and other debilitating diseases have been inspired by her and learned how to better care of themselves, mentally, physically, and spiritually. Kris is also member of Oprah's SuperSoul 100, recognizing the most influential thought leaders today and was named a role model by *The New York Times.* Her book *Crazy Sexy Diet* was a New York Times best seller and number one Amazon best seller.

Kris Carr is saying live a life that is crazy and sexy. Kris's beauty is evident both inside and out. Her optimism is apparent in all that she does. She inspires inner strength by proclaiming that we should all get up each day and perform at a high level.

Today, 17 years later, Kris is still living with her diagnosis and leading a full life. She regularly lectures at hospitals, wellness centers, and corporations, and has even lectured at Harvard University. She launched a wellness website that has a following of over 40,000 people. She is celebrated as one of the most prominent experts on heathy living. I encourage you to visit her website at kriscarr.com.

Kris could have accepted her diagnosis and become negative and resigned to her fate. If she had done that, she would probably not be alive today. Because Kris decided to live fully with a heart of optimism she has transformed her life and is now helping thousands transform their own lives.

Both Granny and Kris were given raw deals. My Granny lived in an abusive household and in poverty. At her lowest point, though, she was given the strength to change her life. Kris was living a life full of promise. It took courage and optimism for her to not be defeated by her grim diagnosis. We all have bad days and even bad years. It is up to each of us to decide to change the negative in our lives to positives. Live fully like Granny and Kris. Live with a heart of optimism.

Questions:

1. What was the lowest point of your life? How did you handle it?
2. Do you consider yourself an optimistic person?
3. Do you feel like optimism helps, even when it may not be realistic?

Heart of Creativity
R.G. LeTourneau

"Imagination is the beginning of creation. You imagine what you desire,
you will what you imagine, and at last, you create what you will"
- George Bernard Shaw

My father was in the military and I was a military brat, moving from place to place. While on vacation, we would often visit my grandfather and it was always a unique experience. He was so creative and had a way of working with iron that was distinctive and special. His hands, callused and hardened, told the story of his many creations.

My grandfather was one of the designers for The Coors manufacturing plant in Golden, Colorado. My mother used to tell us how he helped build the railings that the bottles traveled on from fill to distribution within the plant. My grandfather's creations were not limited to work; he created an amazingly intricate iron table for my mother. The iron was bent and shaped in many variations, each bend a testament to his talent. The table had a glass top and the table itself was made of hard rod iron.

 I did not inherit any of the creative genes in my family, but I admire those who did. My brother Troy and Uncle Mike are both incredibly creative. While in high school, Troy won a statewide art competition. He can draw and weld and is one of the most creative people I know. After struggling with alcoholism for years, my Uncle Mike found his salvation in his creativity. He designed and created the interior faux gold marble for the state capitol of Colorado. His creations are a main feature of the capital building. Creative people like my grandfather, brother and uncle have helped to shape our world. Each unique creation they share is a story into their lives.

R.G. LeTourneau was a man with a heart for creativity. His inventions literally helped to pave America. His faith helped to guide his calling and he became known as one of the most influential businessmen in the world.

R.G. was not born into a creative household, he had to hone his skills over many years, trials, and failures. He dropped out of school in the sixth grade and dropped into manual labor. At only 14, he got his first job at an iron foundry making metal castings. This type of work is hard, dangerous, and labor intensive. R.G. would pour molten metals into castings to form the shapes required. Once cooled, he would remove the hardened metal shape from the molds.

While working at the foundry, R.G. developed a reputation at being good with machines. We can find our gift at young age if we allow our heart and minds to be open to it, but R.G. wasn't ready. He moved from one job to another, developing his skills along the way. He traveled to the west coast and took jobs as a woodcutter, brick layer, miner, battery refurbisher, carpenter and eventually as a welder at the Buena Vista Power Plant. He held jobs in many different areas of construction and building. His creative nature began to take shape. He began to understand how the materials to build worked in conjunction with the machinery.

R.G.'s heart of creativity led him to San Francisco, where he worked as a welder. He was there during the great earthquake of 1906 and survived with a broken neck. A decade later, he barely escaped the Spanish Influenza outbreak that killed millions worldwide. A devout Christian, he felt that his faith allowed him to survive these extreme events and once stated that his faith allowed "all my bitterness to drain away."

During his extraordinary travels and numerous jobs RG decided to take a correspondence course in mechanics. Once he completed the course, he designed a final exam for himself, disassembling and rebuilding a motorcycle he had purchased. When asked about his education in later life, he would often joke he had a bachelors in motorcycles.

As his skills grew, people and businesses began to seek him out. It was not until he was tasked with clearing 40 acres of land by Holt Manufacturing that he finally discovered his true calling. He enjoyed the work so much he decided to buy his own Holt Tractor and start his own trucking and earth moving business. It would seem to be terrible timing, as it was in the midst of the Great Depression. But R.G. was guided by his faith and dedicated to becoming God's businessman. When most businesses were floundering and struggling, R. G's business exploded. FDR's New Deal provided earth moving businesses opportunities such as the Hoover Dam, Boulder Highway, and Orange County Dam. R.G.'s company benefited from the building boom.

R.G's fortunes took another positive turn when he decided to stop trucking and start designing and building earth moving equipment of his own. His equipment was revolutionary for its time. He designed low-pressure tires which were better equipped at handling tough terrain. He invented the bulldozer and tournapull (two-wheeled tractors) and he was the first to create off-shore drilling platforms. Like most creative people, he could visualize a future before it materialized. At the height of his career he had over 300 patents to his name.

R.G. was a successful inventor, but he not immune to failure. He had to often persuade banks to be patient and give him a little longer to pay off his debts.

An epic world historic event would help cement the company's success. During World War II, his factories supplied LeTourneau machines to the Allied forces, making up nearly 70 percent of the earth moving equipment used during the war. When the war ended, LeTourneau built a school to educate veterans and promote technical and engineering education.

R.G.'s heart of creativity helped to shape the landscape of America and the world. He was guided by his faith but his calling was pure and he found his happiness in building and creating machinery.

The LeTourneau company has over four manufacturing plants in Texas along with the school he built. R.G. was a humble man who gave more than he took. He and his family lived off ten percent of the revenue his companies brought in and the other 90 percent was donated or given to away to promote his Christian faith and support the school and its education of future innovative thinkers.

R.G. LeTourneau's was a heart of creativity and a testament to the power of finding and following our calling. When we do that, we can move our world. R.G. not only moved his world, but helped propel it forward into the future.

Questions:

1. Do you consider yourself a creative person? Why or why not?
2. Do you feel that you have a calling? What is it?
3. Do you think RG's philanthropy is extreme? What is your approach to your own personal philanthropy?

Heart of Action
Amelia Earhart

*"The path to success is to take massive,
determined action."*
- Tony Robbins

When I was in high-school I dreamed of leaving my hometown of Robertsdale, Alabama. I felt the only thing for me in Robertsdale was trouble and a long life of construction work. I joined the army in 1988 and was sent to Fort Sill, Oklahoma for boot camp and advanced training. After boot camp, I received my orders to go to Germany. I arrived in Germany in January 1989. It was cold and beautiful. I was not scared but I was lonely, having just left my family and friends for the foreseeable future. Yet what I had done was act. I was bound and determined to live a life that was not confined to Robertsdale or controlled by others but was dictated by my desires and dreams. I acted! -

As we grow older we sometimes lose our heart to take action. I know through my own personal transformation that I had lost my heart of action for a while. Now that I have regained it, I am doing more, becoming more, and experiencing more adventures than I have in years. My life is more enjoyable and fulfilling all because I have taken action.

Amelia Earhart was a person of action. She lived her life to the very end owning her dreams and desires. Amelia defied the perceived notions of the day. She wanted to fly even though there were not many licensed female pilots in the 1920's. One study stated there may have been as few as sixteen. Flying and piloting was for men. Amelia had other plans though. As history showed, she was a woman of action.

Amelia had a sense of adventure early on. As a child, she and her sister often set out on adventures catching bugs, running through the neighborhood, and even shooting rats. Amelia was the ringleader, talking her younger sister into these crazy adventures. She was the quintessential tomboy before the word tomboy was used. Ever the adventurer, she wanted to add flying to her growing list of exploits.

With the help of her uncle, in 1904, Amelia put together a homemade ramp fashioned after a roller coaster she had seen on a trip to St. Louis. She secured the ramp to the roof of the family toolshed. This was her well-documented first flight and it ended in dramatic fashion. Amelia emerged from the broken wooden box that had served as a sled, exhilarated, with a bruised lip and a torn dress. She told her sister Pidge it was just like flying.

At the Iowa State Fair, Amelia saw her first airplane, though she later described it as a rust bucket that seemed to be falling apart. Her father offered to have her and her sister take a flight, but they wisely chose to go back to the merry-go-round.

For Amelia, life was grand except for the turmoil her father put the family through. He was an alcoholic who lost his job at the railroad in 1914. Under duress at home and with an adventurer's spirit, she began her call to action. Throughout her troubled childhood, Amelia aspired to something more, keeping a scrapbook of successful women working in male-dominated fields, including law, film production, mechanical engineering, advertising, and management. She even left one high school to attend another because the chemistry department was better. Amelia graduated high-school in 1916 from Chicago's Hyde Park High School.

During a trip to visit her sister in Toronto in 1917, Amelia was dramatically affected by the wounded soldiers returning from World War I. These men did not just return with physical injuries, they also returned with what was then known as shell shock. Amelia felt compelled to help and trained to become a nurse's aide with the Red Cross. Amelia began her work with the voluntary aid detachment at a military hospital.

In 1918, an outbreak of the Spanish Flu decimated the hospital staff, so Amelia worked extremely hard, taking extra shifts and additional duties. She contracted pneumonia, which was compounded by serious sinus issues. She spent the next year recovering and living with her sister.

When her strength returned, she began pursuing her dreams and living her call to action. She began her studies at Columbia University as a pre-med student, but dropped out after just a year. In December of 1920, she took her first airplane ride in California with famous World War I pilot Frank Hawks. She was forever hooked.

Amelia began taking flying lessons in 1921 from a female flight instructor named Neta Snook. To pay for these lessons she worked as a filing clerk at the Los Angeles Telephone Company. Amelia passed her flight test in December 1921, earning her National Aeronautics Association License. She then bought her first plane a second-hand Kinner Airster, which she nicknamed, The Canary. Two days after the purchase she participated in her first flight exhibition at the Sierra Airdrome in Pasadena, California.

Amelia's heart of action led her to set many aviation records. Her first flying record was in 1922 when she became the first woman to fly solo above 14,000 feet.

In 1931, Amelia married American publisher George Putnam, who helped promote her amazing feats. A year later, she became the first woman and only the second person after Charles Lindbergh to fly solo across the Atlantic Ocean. Amelia flew out of Newfoundland, Canada on May 20th in a Lockheed Vega 5B and landed in a cow field near Londonderry, Ireland.

When Amelia returned from her transatlantic flight, Congress awarded her the Distinguished Flying Cross, a military decoration awarded for extraordinary achievement while participating in aerial flight. Amelia was in the boy's club and was being recognized for her daring spirit. Flight was still in its infancy in those days, so every time she left the ground in her yellow airplane she was in a position to set records or do something few had done. Because of her transatlantic trip and newly found fame, she spent a lot of time on speaking tours and raising money for her next big goal of circumnavigating the globe.

Amelia began her preparations for her global trip in 1937. After a failed first attempt, she and navigator Fred Noonan departed from Oakland, California. After 40 days and more than 20 stops they arrived in Papua New Guinea. On July 2, they began their hardest leg of their journey, a 2,500-mile trip to Howland Island, their next refueling stop. They never made it.

Amelia was never heard from again. Her legend, however, has never been silenced and over 80 year later her story still captures our imagination. Her passion for flying helped popularize aviation while in its infancy and opened doors for women. Amelia challenged the status quo and got to live her dreams of flying. She was singularly focused on a dream and pursued it with a relentless heart of action.

Questions:

1. Is there an action you are afraid to take right now?
2. What's the worst thing that would happen if you took that action?
3. Have you ever been a first in anything you've done?

Heart of Invention
Madam CJ Walker | Hedy LaMarr

*"Nothing in life is to be feared, it is only to be understood.
Now is the time to understand more, so that we may fear less."*
- Marie Curie

My friend, Roy, had the knack of taking things apart and putting them back together just to see how they worked. He once took an old lawnmower engine he had found in his yard and, using some junk he found lying around, made a small, motorized scooter. He was adept at identifying problems and then finding a solution to those problems. That's the kind of skill inventors have. If they can find an easier way to do something to improve their lives or the lives of others, they do it.

I have never had an inventive side. I am more of a fixer. The problems I identify deal with building teams and leadership within teams. I know how to get people to work together to improve on projects. Sarah Breedlove and Hedy LaMarr were inventers who took extreme situations and found solutions.

Sarah, who is better known as Madam C.J. Walker, knew how to invent and bring teams together to better her world and the lives of African American women. She invented products and found ways to market those products. Sarah changed her world both personally and financially but she also changed the world of African American women throughout the United States, South America, and the Caribbean.

Sarah had a heart for invention. She was born to uneducated sharecroppers in 1867 in the Louisiana Delta, where both of her parents had once been slaves before the Civil War. Sarah was orphaned at age seven. According to Sarah, "I got my start by giving myself a start." She and her sister survived by working in the cotton fields in Vicksburg, Mississippi. These were not easy times to be a black person in America, especially in the south. At 14, Sarah married a man named Moses McWilliams just to escape the abuse by her brother-in-law Jesse Powell.

Moses and Sarah had a child together named Lelia, later known as A'Lelia Walker, who born June 6, 1885. Two years after her birth, Moses died, and Sarah had to find a way to survive. She moved to St. Louis to join her four brothers who had all found careers as barbers. Sarah wanted to educate her daughter, so she got a job as a laundress making only $1.50 a day. This provided her with the means to make sure A'Lelia got a public school education.

Sarah began settling into life in St. Louis and developed friendships with other black women in her community. Friendships and the freedom of enjoying everyday life were not what Sarah or many black Americans were used to. Slavery had only been abolished a couple of decades earlier and many black Americans still had to deal with the restrictions created by Jim Crow laws and racism.

Sarah's fortunes would begin to change when she developed a scalp condition which caused her hair to fall out. Sarah went to her brothers and a black female entrepreneur named Annie Malone for guidance. Annie was a chemist who developed and sold products for black women. Sarah began selling products for Annie and moved to Denver with her daughter.

After marrying Charles Joseph Walker, she moved back to St. Louis and started her own business. Sarah told people she had a dream for a healing formula for scalp conditioning and hair growth, and this caused her to break off from Annie and create her own product line. Sarah changed her name to Madam C.J. Walker and her fortunes began to quickly change.

Madam C.J. Walker spent nearly two years traveling the southern states, south America, and the Caribbean promoting and marketing her products. Contrary to some sources, Madam Walker never invented chemical perms or a straightening comb. What she did do was invent products and create marketing programs that were similar to Avon today. Can you imagine traveling the southern states as a black woman during Jim Crow? Walker was passionate and her heart for invention drove her success.

In 1910, Madam Walker settled in Indianapolis, which was the nation's largest manufacturing center. She donated money to open a YMCA devoted to colored people in the city. Her daughter moved to Harlem and opened the upscale Madam C.J. Walker Salon. Madam Walker once wrote to lawyer F. B. Ransom that her establishment rivaled the salons on Fifth Avenue.

In 1916, she moved to Harlem and left the business operations to F.B. Ransom and Alice Kelly. But that didn't mean she was idle. Madam Walker always had something new to create or work toward. She took special interest in the NAACP's anti-lynching movement and contributed $5000 to the cause, an enormous amount for the day. She even visited the White House in 1917 to promote an anti-lynching campaign.

As her business thrived she decided to hold a business convention for black women in Philadelphia to celebrate her sales agents and those who worked in her salons. This was the first convention for female black entrepreneurs in the United States. Madam Walker had a way of identifying problems and finding solutions. By the time of her death in 1919, her company was worth well over one million dollars. Accounting for inflation, that would be nearly $26 million in 2020 dollars. A century later, Walker's life became the inspiration for a Netflix series, *Self Made*, starring Octavia Spencer.

Walker's heart of invention helped black American women feel and look beautiful. Her products ushered in a change for women who were the first descendants of freed slaves. At her convention in Philadelphia she told the delegates, "This is the greatest country under the sun."

Despite being born to freed slaves and dealing with extreme racism, she was able to live the American Dreams. At the end of her life she stated, "There is no royal flower-strewn path to success…and if there is, I have not found it for if I have accomplished anything in life it is because I have been willing to work hard." Her heart of invention led her to amazing success. In addition to the Netflix docudrama, she has also been the subject of many books.

Walker's heart of invention was not limited to products. She also developed new marketing strategies. Her success was achieved without a formal education. She inspired women throughout the United States to work hard to escape their living conditions. If you ever thought you could not rise above your circumstances because of your environment or a modest upbringing, look to Madam C.J. Walker for inspiration. Her life was one of invention.

Hedy LaMarr was best known as a movie star and one of the most beautiful women in the world. She never had to struggle like Sarah Breedlove, but her beauty, and the fact she was a woman, hindered her ability to try and help the allies during World War II.

LaMarr was an actress during the 1930s and 1940's where she played in Oscar-nominated films such as *Algiers*, and *Sampson and Delilah*. However, her greatest legacy was not her beauty or fame, it was her mind and technical ability.

LaMarr was born in Austria to Jewish parents. Early on she exhibited a brilliant mind, but her beauty took center stage. She studied acting and landed a few stage and film roles. She was married at nineteen to an older man who was wealthy and domineering. Hedy fled her unhappy situation on a bicycle in the middle of the night and eventually ended up in London.

In London, Hedy met Louis B. Mayer, the infamous MGM studio head. Though not being fluent in English, LaMarr somehow talked her way into a Hollywood contract. Settling in Beverly Hills life she began socializing with the elite, including Howard Hughes and John F. Kennedy. Hedy was not only beautiful she had a mind that wanted to invent and perform scientific experiments.

For a time, she dated Hughes, who encouraged her scientific pursuits. When Hedy was not acting, she was working with experiments in her studio provided trailer. She had found her calling in that environment. Hedy once told a journalist, "Inventions are easy for me to do. I don't have to work on ideas, they come naturally to me."

Hedy's desire to experiment and invent led her to work another innovative soul named George Antheil. They both were concerned about the looming war and began to tinker with ideas to combat the axis powers. They filed a patent to protect radio communications for the Allies. It was a device for frequency hopping. This prevented allied torpedoes from being detected by the Nazis. While it wasn't implemented by the Navy during WWII the technology formed the basis for today's Wi-Fi, Bluetooth and GPS systems

Hedy's inventions were never as recognized as her movie career. The U.S. military has publically acknowledged her patent and contribution to technology but she was never truly recognized for her amazing inventions.

In 1997, Hedy became the first female awarded the BULBIE Gnass Spirit of Achievement Award, which many consider the Oscars for inventing. Hedy received many accolades throughout her life for her beauty and her movies but this accolade was for her invention.

Not everyone has the desire or ability to invent something that solves problems or makes lives better. We do, however, have the ability to change ourselves, to reinvent ourselves for the better.

Both Madam C.J. Walker and Hedy LaMarr lived to create and invent. One helped usher in the idea of female black entrepreneurs and the other defied the expectation that a woman could either possess extraordinary beauty or extraordinary intelligence. Although their paths were different, they both have unexpectedly changed our world, all because they led lives with a heart of invention.

Questions:

1. Have you ever had an idea that you thought would make a great invention? What stopped you from developing it?
2. Have you ever had to reinvent yourself? Why?
3. Have you ever been underestimated? What did you do about it?

CHAPTER 3

PURSUING A PURPOSE

Heart of Gentleness
Therese Martin

"Only the weak are cruel. Gentleness can only
be expected from the strong."
- Leo Buscaglia

I arrived in Germany in January 1989 at the ripe old age of 18. When I see pictures of myself back then, I see a young and inexperienced kid. As a new soldier in a new land surrounded by tough men I thought I was supposed to be tough. More often than not, I am sure I at least acted that way.

My first weekend in Germany was spent drinking way too much beer and whiskey. While I was too young to drink in the United States, this southern boy was suddenly of legal drinking age in Germany! The guys in my unit were in the same position – young, but legally able to drink and we took full advantage. I spent my first three days in Germany drunk and vomiting. Monday would be a different story as I would be expected to show up and do my duty. I would also be introduced to a man who made a lifelong impact on me.

I was assigned to Sgt. Bill Beam's team. In the Army, you call everyone especially senior leadership by their last names. Not to be disrespectful, I called Bill Sgt. Beam. He looked and acted nothing like the stereotypical tough army sergeant. My first day, I'm sure I looked young and hungover, but Sgt. Beam spoke softly and did not judge me for the weekend's exploits. He could empathize with me. He was once a young soldier himself who partied too much, drank too much, and fought too much. While Sgt. Beam seemed old to me, he was only 25. But when you are 18 and stationed in Germany, anyone over the age of twenty-two seems old.

We would spend the next 90 days in the woods playing army games or doing maneuvers. As a forward observer attached out to army scout units and infantry units I had to be tough or at least act the part. My job was to blow up the enemy by calling in air strikes or artillery fire. We did this by locating the enemy and then coordinating the grid coordinates on the enemies' position.

During this time, I realized that the Army has tough and rugged individuals but the Army also has gentle, loving, and caring individuals like Sgt. Beam. He was exactly what I needed during this time in my life. His wisdom far exceeded his years. He and wife decided early in their marriage to stop partying and to start attending church. This brought them closer together and changed him profoundly.

Sgt. Beam and I shared our life stories. He told me about his abusive father and about helping a lady who had been raped and left to die. He also explained that he wanted to leave the army and become a nurse. While the army had helped him escape his abusive family, now he loathed the thought of hurting people. He only wanted to help them. He had a gentle spirit and wanted peace in his life. His love for God never wavered.

Sgt. Beam lived his faith and did so without judgement of others. He was a wonderful example of what we are all capable of if we truly believe and love. Sgt. Beam always treated us younger soldiers with dignity and respect. He was not one to raise his voice, instead his peaceful commanding presence drew us to him. I learned so much about life during that 90 days. More than anything, I learned that the best example of character is to live it not speak it.

Sgt. Beam would be in my life for only six more months and then he left the Army. When he left, I cried because he had such a profound effect on me when I needed it most. Sgt. Beam's example of peace and love are forever etched in my soul. I recently caught up with his wife on Facebook. This gentle man of peace became a nurse. I am certain he still radiates a spirit of peace and loves as he delivers care to all his patients.

Therese Martin was one whose example of gentleness and love led her to sainthood in the Catholic Church. St. Therese of Lisieux lived a modest life as a nun, but she is most known for her biography, *A Story of a Soul*, which was published after her death. This spiritual classic is still in print, a century after its publication. Its main message is that ordinary people could live saintly lives without doing heroic acts of valor.

Therese Martin was born in 1873 in France, the youngest of nine children to religious parents. Her father was a watchmaker and she adored and felt protected by her mother. Therese childhood was full of loss, however. Four of her siblings died as children. Her beloved mother also died when she was only four and an older sister who cared for her left to join the nunnery.

As the baby of the family, Therese was precocious and sensitive and prone to emotional outbursts. The rest of the family babied Therese and doted on her. What made her different was that from the age of nine she knew her calling was to be a nun. Her father even recognized her passion and desire to serve the Lord.

At the age of 14, Therese had a conversion experienced that transformed her life and she began her quest to become a nun. The church leaders would not allow it until she was older. The main priest of her church told her she could not do so until she was 21. She then asked the bishop who affirmed the local priest's ruling.

Her father strongly believed in his daughter's calling and decided to take her on a pilgrimage to meet and appeal to Pope Leo XIII. Therese sat in on a mass and she was filled with emotion and love. After the mass, she waited patiently to kiss the feet of Pope Leo and to ask the question. Finally, she was up, and bent down to kiss the Pope's feet and then grabbed his hands and asked him earnestly if she could join the nunnery. Can you imagine how brave she must have been at 14 years old? For most people, talking to the Pope wasn't even considered. They just kissed his feet and moved along.

The Pope turned her down, but Therese persisted with her voice trembling and possibly even begging. The pope's guards eventually had to drag her away as tears streamed down her face. This persistence eventually paid off though, when she was granted permission to join the convent at age 16.

Some of the other nuns were jealous and considered her professed love of God fake. They did not know she was writing about her daily life and how much she loved the Lord. They had no idea how she lived each day with an unshakable confidence in God's love.

Therese had experienced so much pain as a child and was sickly herself. She had endured the loss of mother and siblings as a child. She even watched and witnessed her father slowly struggle with pain and be put in a mental institution. But she never wavered in her love for God. Her focus was on doing the ordinary with extraordinary love. Through it all, she devoted herself to peace and love.

Though young, her own health was failing and Therese died at the age of 24 of tuberculosis. Her last words were simple, "My God, I love you." Before she died she stated she would not be known until after her death.

A year later, her autobiography, *A Story of a Soul*, was published. She described that it is not great deeds, but great love that make us strong. She loved flowers and saw herself as the "little flower" of Jesus and she is often referred to that way. Her autobiography led to her canonization in 1924.

During WWI and World War II, St. Therese of Lisieux was known as the patron saint of soldiers, as many carried pictures of her to keep them out of harm's way. Had she lived to 1924 when she was sainted she would have only been 52 years old. Her mission was to make God loved! How powerful, is that? From the age of nine she knew her calling. She knew she lived for peace and love and was inspired to change the world just by being gentle and loving.

I imagine Sgt. Beam does that every day, tending to patients and providing his peaceful voice of love and care without judgment. St. Therese of Lisieux did not judge, she just loved God fully, inspiring millions to the do the same long after she had passed.

Questions:

1. 1. Was there someone who influenced your life greatly when you were young? Who was it?
2. 2. Do you agree or disagree that gentleness can only be expected from the strong? Why?
3. 3. Did you have a conviction when you were young that carried through to adulthood?

Heart of Freedom
William Carney

"The great revolution in the history of man, past, present and future,
is the revolution of those determined to be free."
- John F. Kennedy

What drives you to perform at your very best? What are you so passionate about that you would be willing to give your life for it? In high school, I played football and when we were training and practicing with team members everyone worked toward a common goal - to win at all cost. Some days after practice my muscles were sore and I ached all over. While I would leave practice on these days and head home to do homework and get ready for the next day, my heart and mind were still on the practice field. I always felt as if I did not give my all and that was the case how was that affecting my team?

I was not good at a lot of things in school. Academically, I was middle of the pack at best. Football, though, was something else. I was considered good by coaches and teammates. One coach told me he had never coached anyone who worked so hard during practice. He often told me I practiced every day as if I was in game. His words would make me want to practice even harder.

I felt that by practicing hard and working hard at football I could somehow escape my personal conflicts. It was my way to freedom. My parents had divorced, which devastated me. On the weekends when I was not able to practice football, I would be out drinking when I got off work at Greer's grocery store, where I worked part-time as stock clerk. While maybe this helped me escape a little, it sometimes made me feel worse. But football was freedom and I relished every moment.

When football was over after my senior season I had to find a new outlet. I knew I wanted to get out of my small town, so I joined the Army. While you think of the military as being structured and rigid, and it is, it was there where I discovered my personal freedom. I realized after serving in Desert Storm that I wanted to be a teacher and help others. Knowing what I wanted to do with my life was freeing to me. My heart of freedom was in helping others and teaching.

William Carney discovered his heart of freedom seeking freedom. William was the ultimate patriot and he received the country's highest military honor for it. Of the nearly 3500 American soldiers who have ever been awarded the Medal of Honor, only 88 have been African Americans. Sgt. William Carney was the first one to receive that high honor.

William was born into slavery in Norfolk, Virginia in 1840, and his family were eventually granted freedom by their slave owners. William's parents moved the family to Massachusetts, which was more accepting of freed slaves than southern states and seemed a good starting place for the family. William had a desire for an education even though the laws of the day prohibited blacks from learning to read and write. He also had a strong desire to become a preacher and to serve God whom he felt led his family to freedom. His plans quickly changed when the Civil War broke out. He now felt he could serve God best by serving by joining the Union Army .

Keep in mind, that unlike the African Americans in the south, William was already a free man. His freedom had been won. Still, perhaps he felt called to join the fight to help end slavery. By doing so he was certainly endangering his life. Had he or his fellow black soldiers been captured while fighting in the south there is no telling what treatment they would have received at the hands of Confederate soldiers.

William joined the Massachusetts famed 54th infantry regiment of the Union Army in 1863. This was the country's first all-black unit. He was quickly sent off to training. The exploits of the 54th Army Regiment loosely served as inspiration for the 1989 movie, Glory featuring Denzel Washington. Williams trained alongside the sons of Frederick Douglas, the famous abolitionist. After several months of training his unit of 45 other African Americans were sent war.

During the unit's first major combat mission in Charleston, South Carolina on July 18, 1863, the 54th regiment led the charge on Fort Wagner. This was hardly considered an honor. The northern commanders felt they could weaken Fort Wagner's strong hold and force it to use many of its stored munitions by sending in the all black unit first. Basically, the 54th regiment was a sacrificial lamb. It was during this battle, though, that William would become a true hero to all and help ignite the passions of African Americans throughout the union.

During the battle, the unit color guard was shot. Seeing the man stumble and the flag begin to fall, William rushed to catch it. Just before the flag hit the ground, he held it up high for all to see.

The importance of the colors, or the flag, cannot be truly understood in today's technologically advanced military. In the Civil War, however, and most armed combat of the era, the colors were instrumental in winning or losing battles. They were a way to communicate as there were no radios or computers. If the flag was going left, the troops knew to go left. In this case, the flag was charging up the beach head toward Fort Wagner. Had the flag fallen to the ground it may have caused the troop to become confused.

In the heat of live combat, the flurry of flying bullets and cannon fire can become extremely overwhelming. This is why the colors were so important. The colors symbolized team, unit designations, and country. William was fighting for all of them. His was a heart of freedom.

William grabbed the flag just before it hit the ground and then proceeded toward Fort Wagner. As he moved toward the fort, he was shot several times. He suffered gunshot wounds to the head, legs, and hip. Not once did he drop the colors. As he lost blood he fell to his knees and continued to crawl and claw his way up the beachhead. Many fellow soldiers later said that even though William was seriously wounded, he continued to courageously urge the men forward.

Clinging tightly to the colors, William finally planted the flag at the base of the fort. He refused to let go despite his wounds. He would just hold the flag tighter if his fellow soldiers tried to relieve him. As he was bleeding out and nearly faint he finally released the colors only after they were safe, crying out, "Boys, the old flag never touched the ground!"

William nearly died from his wounds. Once he made it to the military hospital, which was probably a clearing in the woods, it was discovered that he had at least four gunshot wounds. One bullet could not be removed and he lived with the pain for the remainder of his life. Two months after the charge on Fort Wagner the Union Army was finally victorious. For his daring, William was promoted to sergeant. More than 35 years later, on May 23, 1900 he was awarded the Medal of Honor, the highest award our nation has to offer.

William Carney was a person who had a heart of freedom. He was willing to give his life so others could experience the same freedom he enjoyed living in Massachusetts. When I fought in Desert Storm, I found my own personal freedom by discovering my calling. Freedom is not just words written in the constitution. Freedom is what we make of it. For me it was becoming an educator. I have never doubted my decision and it has brought me years of joy. For William, it was literally fighting for the freedom of others. When we stay true to our heart and our calling, we discover real freedom. Live life with a heart of freedom.

Questions:

1. What does freedom mean to you?
2. Is there anything you are so passionate about that you would be willing to give your life for it?
3. What gives you a sense of freedom?

Heart of Determination
Greta Thunberg

"You are successful the moment you start
moving toward a worthwhile goal."
- Charles Carlson

How determined are you? When I was in third grade I was often bullied, and picked on by the other children because I could not read very well. I was tested and placed in special classes for reading and math. I was miserable and embarrassed and would often try to cheat on spelling tests and find ways around my academic lessons so I did not feel dumb in front of my classmates.

But I was determined to learn how to read on grade level. My journey was personal. I did not have to share my goal with anyone.. I would stay up late at night practicing my reading skills and doing homework, which was not easy for me. My parents would try to help me, but I still spent many nights working on homework by myself late into the evening. It took me nearly six years, but by the end of my eighth-grade year I finally tested on level.

Even as an adult with a master's degree, I struggle with comprehension. I learn best by listening and doing. But when we are determined, we can conquer our fears and achieve our goals. Greta Thunberg has found her heart of determination. At just 15 years old, she has made it her cause to speak up for climate change. Greta has not just become a vocal advocate, she has become, in the words of author Margaret Atwood, "The Joan of Arc" for climate change. What started as a one child protest at the doorsteps of the Swedish Parliament has grown to a worldwide cause.

As a middle age male nearing 50, I can't imagine having the nerve to do this, but I admire her determination to stand for something. Greta is on the autism spectrum, and has been diagnosed with Asperger's, which is characterized by difficulties in social interaction and nonverbal communication, along with a laser focus on certain topics. Greta does not see this diagnosis as a hindrance to her cause, however. If anything, she feels this is her superpower.

In fact, Tony Attwood, a world authority on Asperger's, has said people diagnosed are "usually renowned for being direct, speaking their mind and being honest and determined and having a strong sense of social justice."

When you hear Greta speak, her disorder is evident. But what is also evident is her singular determination. This one-person protest has turned into an international awakening. Greta has spoken at the United Nations. She has been courted by heads of state. Greta has even traded jabs with Donald Trump because of her climate change efforts. Greta is the youngest person to ever be nominated for a Nobel Prize.

True determination can change our world. It certainly completely changed Greta's. She inspired four million to strike for climate change in September 2019. I was determined to just read on grade level and I thought that was daunting. Yet this young teenage girl was determined to change the world!

Greta's voice is powerful and full of determination. Invited to speak to group of world leaders, Greta boldly spoke these words, "You have stolen my dreams and my childhood with your empty words. And yet I'm one of the lucky ones. People are suffering. People are dying. Entire ecosystems are collapsing," she said. "We are in the beginning of a mass extinction, and all you can talk about is money and fairy tales of eternal economic growth. How dare you!" Can you imagine talking to your parents with such boldness, much less a group of world leaders? This is where her Asperger's probably becomes her superpower. Greta's weakness is her strength. With determination Greta proclaims it is time for the world to change.

As a child, I was determined to read on level with my peers and overcome my fear of feeling dumb in front of my classmates. Yet as an adult, I have spent many years living in fear. What happened? You may say because it is easier to be fearless when you are young. But now as a middle-aged man, I am determined to live my dreams and to pursue all my goals with exuberance. As my determination has grown so has my ability to step forward and face the things that once scared me. When we live life with a heart of determination we can truly change our personal world and overcome our fears.

A dear friend of mine, Gayle, went through a divorce a few years ago. She had been with a man who seldom put her first and made her feel her aspirations were unimportant. That was apparent in a story she shared with me that occurred during their second year of marriage and had a profound effect on her.

While living in the Mississippi Delta. Gayle and her husband attended a balloon festival. He was offered a ride in one of the balloons and while there was plenty of room, he did not offer to have her join him. Instead she watched the balloon float away across a beautiful sky. But Gayle was happy for her husband and just accepted it as a gesture from one friend to another.

However, when the couple arrived at home that night, she asked him why he had not invited her to go on the balloon ride. He said, "you cannot ride in my balloon," a selfish comment that stung and had a lasting effect.

Gayle was not originally from the Mississippi Delta and often felt like an outsider. Her husband's family were wealthy and had expectations that Gayle should serve as an old-fashioned southern wife. That meant she was to raise the children, cook, keep the house, be a member of women's auxiliaries, and carry herself with the grace and charm befitting her husband's status. As this was Gayle's second marriage, she was determined to do all she could to make it work.

Gayle finished her bachelor's degree and started teaching public school, a job she loved. But her in-laws felt teaching at a public school was beneath her and offered to help her get a job at a prominent private school in the Mississippi Delta. But Gayle was determined to keep her position and remained at the public school.

When her boys were born, she was devoted to their upbringing and happiness and life was good. Gayle and her husband moved from the confines of the Mississippi Delta to Gulfport, Mississippi. Her career as an educator was flourishing. One day she came home and her husband informed her they were moving to Arizona. She was not given a choice. Gayle felt her husband was jealous of her success as an educator.

After a couple of years, the family moved to northern Alabama. Her husband abruptly left her and the kids. She was stuck in a place where she had few friends and few opportunities, only a house to live in that was given to her by her in-laws.

Gayle was determined not to stay there, however. She loved her time in Gulfport and made some calls to old colleagues. She was soon offered a job and sold the house and, with her youngest son – her oldest was away in college - moved back to the Mississippi coast. Gayle was determined to find her joy again and to share that joy with her boys, who had seen her suffer and endure their father's selfish behavior for many years.

It is hard to live with a heart of determination. We get intimidated or feel trapped by life's circumstances. Greta, Gayle and I had to find our own paths and live with a heart of determination to fulfill our goals. Greta is determined to bring climate change concerns to the world and hopefully make a lasting change to save our climate. Gayle was determined to find her own way and live the statement, "I have my own balloon." As for me, I am determined not to let fear derail my dreams. Live with a heart of determination. When you do you can change your world and the world around you.

Questions:

1. Do you consider yourself to be a determined person? Why?
2. Can you list an example where your determination influenced an outcome?
3. What does it mean to you to "have your own balloon?"

Heart of a Champion
Buster Douglas

*"Champions are made from something they have deep
inside of them-a desire, a dream, a vison."*
- Mahatma Gandhi

My mother passed away December 28, 2015. Three years before she went to heaven, she had her leg amputated. She had lived with a leg that was constantly getting infected that caused her severe pain. Before the surgery she looked at my brother and I and told us she wanted to ride a bike when she got better. Though it seemed impossible at the time, that was her goal.

One heavyweight boxer I admire achieved what most considered an impossible goal. Few boxing fans would think of Buster Douglas as a great champion. But what I love about Buster is that for one extraordinary moment, he mustered the will, desire, and motivation to become champion of the world.

How often have we had moments where we had an opportunity to be champion of our world? In my life, I have missed more championship moments because of fear of failure or a lack of will than I care to imagine. The thing about fighters is that they are willing to get in a boxing ring with hundreds, thousands, and even millions watching and face their fears. Even the greatest boxer must summon the nerve to enter this modern-day gladiatorial arena and face an opponent who wants to knock them out and possibly humiliate them with everyone watching.

Buster was scheduled to fight the reigning heavyweight champ, Mike Tyson, in February 1990 in Tokyo. James Buster Douglas vs. Mike Tyson was considered a David and Goliath matchup, just a sparring match for Tyson who was tuning up for a real fight with Evander Holyfield. Mike Tyson had steamed rolled through his opponents on his way to the heavyweight title. He was 37-0 and looked unbeatable. Not many heavyweights ever get the moniker of pound for pound the best boxer in the world, but Mike Tyson did! Buster, on the other hand, was ranked 7th in the world by Ring Magazine. He was no slouch, but was widely predicted to lose to Tyson.

Leading up to the fight, Buster experienced several setbacks, including the death of his beloved mother just 23 days before the big fight. She had been his biggest cheerleader, and before her death had told everyone that her son was going to be champion of the world from the ladies at the local beauty parlor to anyone that would listen. At one point, Buster explained that Mike Tyson was the real deal and that she was embarrassing him going around saying he was going to beat him. But she was proud of her son and certain he'd be the future champion.

Buster also got the flu just days before the fight. Between his mother's death and the flu, he probably could have backed out of the fight. Most of media and boxing aficionados cast him an easy target for Tyson.

Throughout his career, Buster had not always fought with the heart of a champion. His fights were not wonders to behold. Sometimes, though, champions are born out of hardship and trials.

But something changed on this night in February 1990. From the first bell, it was apparent that Buster had come to fight. He was in shape and his eyes were on the prize. It was also apparent that throughout the first few rounds that Tyson was not on his game and was not his usual dominant self. Buster was throwing jabs at Tyson that clearly frustrated him.

In between the third and fourth rounds Tyson's corner man screamed at him to stop just standing in the ring. Throughout the next few rounds, the fighters went back and forth with punches. Buster kept fighting. Unlike many fighters who had faced Tyson, he was not giving up.

At the end of the eighth round with only about 10 seconds left, Tyson caught Buster with one of his signature uppercuts and he fell hard to the mat. This is where the story gets good. Can you imagine all the thoughts and emotions he was experiencing? The memory of burying his mother, who so believed in him, just three weeks earlier. Getting the flu just days before the big fight. All these setbacks and losses standing in his way as the referee counted, "1,2,3…"

But Buster would not be denied and stood up as the bell rang. Who knows what made him pull himself off the mat? I say he fought for something more than himself this night in Tokyo.

As the bell rang for the ninth round, Buster and his corner men knew Tyson would come out swinging hard. They knew he would have to withstand the massive blows thrown by Tyson. Buster not only withstood each punch; he gave it back to Tyson. This approach slowed Tyson's flurry of punches. Near the end of the ninth round, Buster started throwing heavy punches that landed and Tyson was clearly hurt and staggering as the bell rang.

As the tenth round began, the injured Tyson came out and pursued Buster. Buster threw a few jabs before landing an uppercut sending Tyson to the mat as he threw four more punches. Tyson's mouthpiece fell out and as he tried grab it to put it back in his mouth he was counted out. Buster Douglas was the new heavyweight champion of the world.

As Buster's team entered the ring for the celebration that ensued, he was visibly shaken. During the post-fight interview, he was asked how he was able to defeat Goliath. With tears rolling down his face he bellowed, "Because of my mother." Buster was champion because he had a reason to fight. He displayed the heart of a champion because he willed himself to victory. This fight is still considered one of the biggest upsets in sports history.

My mom and her doctor had tried to keep her leg through antibiotics and therapy. Nothing worked and it was time to remove the limb. After surgery, she repeated her goal of riding the bike and my brother and I went along with her.

When mom got home from the hospital she no longer had the pain from the leg haunting her. With the constant infections finally gone, she joined a gym. We thought she would do some water aerobics and just work on her physical strength. My mother had different plans though, she was determined to ride a bike. She started taking boot camp classes. She was doing pushups, sit-ups, and moving well with her prosthetic leg. When I would visit, she would challenge me to a pushup contest. Each time she discussed riding a bike.

My mother called me one morning and announced she had ridden a bike – a stationary bike. I was so proud of her. She too had displayed the heart of a champion. Sadly, my mother died a couple of months later.

Had Buster Douglas not fought with a heart of a champion, he would not have defied the odds to beat Tyson. Had my mother not tried and trained and had only accepted her fate, she would not have achieved her goal.

Buster lost his next fight to Evander Holyfield. But for one fleeting moment in time, he was the heavyweight champion. His desire to see his mother's dream come true helped take him to a new level of performance and that was all that was needed to become the champion of the world. Never give up, take on each obstacle no matter how large or small and attack it with a heart of a champion.

Questions:

1. What have been the biggest trials of your life? How did you pick yourself up off the mat?
2. Have you ever achieved a victory, big or small, while you were under duress? What was it?
3. Who/what inspires you to have a heart of a champion?

Heart of Courage
Rebecca Ding | Demosthenes

"The secret to happiness is freedom;
And the secret to freedom is courage."
- Thucydides

There is no truer test of courage than facing the thing that scares you the most.   I was a military brat. We moved every few years to a new town, state, or country. Often it was in the middle of the school year.

I know now that I was very lucky to get the opportunity to experience the world as I grew up. Even though we did not have much, we saw much. But back then I dreaded those moves. Many military brats transition well. Not me. Because I was so shy, making friends was difficult. Since I was in special education classes it was embarrassing for me to leave the regular room to attend my resource classes.

The hardest time I had was our move from Denver to Alabama in the middle of my seventh-grade year. When I registered for school, I heard the chuckle from a kid laughing at my jeans. They were white and my mother had gotten them at a thrift store. While I thought I looked good in those jeans, I was now mortified and self-conscious and that chuckle stayed with me the rest of the year.

I had very few friends and one particular nemesis, Johnny Shaw, who relentlessly taunted and picked on me. The summer after seventh grade, I decided to do something about it. I saved my allowance and any money I could earn and, like generations of boys before me, ordered the Charles Atlas bodybuilder booklets. These booklets promised kids like me relief from bullies. They were workouts designed to build muscle and confidence.

Each week during the summer I received a new booklet. I did everything each booklet said to do. I did pullups, pushups, sit-ups, lifted weights, and worked on my posture and how I carried myself. During the eight or so weeks between my seventh and eighth grade year I put on ten pounds of muscle.

On the first day of my seventh-grade year at my new school I was laughed at and it ruined my entire school year. On the first day of my eighth-grade year that changed. Johnny Shaw pushed me in the restroom and slammed me against the wall. I pushed back! I not only pushed back, I made it clear that this was not the same old Tony. Johnny tried to intimidate me one more time a few days later, but I pushed back again.

The courage it took for me to stand up for myself was beyond scary. What if that push had set me on a course to another year of failure? I will never know because I faced my fear. I stepped out of my comfort zone and was courageous enough to change my destiny that year.

Suddenly, with my newfound confidence, I made friends. I was invited to parties. Johnny Shaw not only stopped bullying me, he also stopped bullying others. I had spent the entire summer working to improve me. I had worked hard to prepare myself for the new year. It paid off. I became the star football player on my eighth-grade team. I was popular for the first time in my life. At the end of the year I was voted best-dressed. How ironic that the boy who was laughed at for wearing jeans from the thrift store would receive that honor.

When I began ninth grade I experienced a few setbacks, but the attitude I developed in my eighth grade helped build my resilience to deal with them. I had developed a heart of courage.

One of my dear friends has one the truest hearts of courage I have ever seen. Her story amazes and inspires me. Rebecca is from China. She grew up impoverished in a small country town. Her parents were educated, but not wealthy and Rebecca wanted to become educated herself. However, it was during the cultural revolution. Schools were closed and education was devalued. She was bullied as she grew up because of her parent's background.

Her ability to push through the bullying and the challenges she faced as a child truly shaped her drive and personal motivation to escape her situation. When she became an adult, she married and soon became pregnant. Shortly afterward, her college professor husband left China and went to France to pursue a better life for their family. This is when Rebecca's courage was kindled.

Rebecca loved her husband and hoped he would soon have her join him in France. This did not happen because she had a place to live through university housing in China. When her husband didn't return after one year, however, the university made her and her new baby move out. She had no place to go and little hope that her husband would return to support her.

Rebecca and her baby moved in with her parents. She went back and forth between her parents and her in-laws' homes as they tried to help raise the baby. Rebecca loved her husband and just knew he would return. He did, but not until two years had passed.

Still, she felt they could salvage their marriage and could move to one of the bigger cities in China where he could find work. But he had other plans. He soon left Rebecca and their young son again and returned to France. Rebecca was heartbroken, but her belief and desire to save the marriage kept her from seeking a divorce.

As the months passed, Rebecca began finding the courage to move forward. She completed her college degree and became a teacher. Teaching did not pay much so she applied to law school. Although she applied to several schools, she was only barely accepted to one of them. The professors and counselors told her that she would have to work hard if she planned to graduate. Rebecca was determined. The setbacks and failures she had experienced from her husband's abandonment were becoming tools to her success.

Rebecca graduated law school and her husband returned from France after years of being away. Their child was nearly five years old and had no relationship with his father. Rebecca summoned her courage and finally asked for a divorce. She also sought and received child support from her soon-to-be ex-husband.

Work was hard to come by in China, so Rebecca started applying to law schools in America where she believed there would be more opportunities. She was accepted to the University of Alabama School of Law in Tuscaloosa, 7500 miles away. With no prospects for employment, no visa to the United States, and a young son, it seemed she would have to postpone her dreams.

Rebecca was not religious, but had met some Christians in China who began talking to her about God and prayer. She began praying and hoping for a chance to leave China. Her visa was approved. She bought plane tickets to Alabama.

When she arrived in Birmingham, she had no place to go. She called a Christian organization in Tuscaloosa. The organization came and picked her and her son up from the airport. Can you imagine the fear and anxiety she must have felt? Landing in a strange country with no idea how to get housing, food, work, or provide childcare for her son. Also, there was a language barrier. Even today, Rebecca struggles with English fluency.

But Rebecca is one of the strongest women I have ever met. She started law school in Tuscaloosa and the Christian organization helped her find work and housing. She graduated law school and found a job, though the job did not last long and she was let go. Cultural differences were affecting her success as a lawyer in America.

She soon found work again and began living her dreams. Her son has been provided with a better life and recently graduated from the local high school. Rebecca has remarried and started her own law practice in Mobile, Alabama. She epitomizes success and is one of the most courageous individuals I know. She encourages me to live my dreams even when they seem impossible to me.

Demosthenes was a man of courage. His story of triumph over setbacks and physical impediments are true acts of courage. He is known as the greatest orator of the ancient world, the Tony Robbins of his era.

Demosthenes was the son of a wealthy sword maker, who died when he was only seven. His father had left him a large inheritance which his guardians were supposed to use to raise him and help pay for his education.

Unlike your typical physical specimen portrayed in Greek statues, Demosthenes was born sickly and frail. He even had a speech impediment, which many people today believe was a lisp or a stutter. The impediment would have hindered his life in ancient Greece.

With his father's wealth, Demosthenes should have been given a great education and a good start in life. However, his unscrupulous guardians stole much of his inheritance and did little to educate him. With little support in regard to education or a proper upbringing, Demosthenes had to make a choice at a young age to make his own way in the world.

Demosthenes would listen to orators and do anything he could to learn about the law. He educated himself. To overcome his speech impediment, he would give full speeches with a pebble in his mouth to strengthen his tongue muscles. He would go to the sea and as the waves crashed against the rocks he would belt out his speeches over and over, so his voice would carry. Demosthenes was growing stronger mentally and finding his voice. To help with his ability to speak fluidly and from his lungs, he ran up hills giving his speeches as he ran. Demosthenes was developing his mind, body, and spirit and a heart of courage.

In Greek culture, there were no lawyers in the court system. Everyone had to represent themselves. Demosthenes used his newfound knowledge and took his guardians to court. He not only took them to court, he won. But there was nothing left of his inheritance. They had squandered it all. Still, the knowledge he gained in court led him to become a prominent orator in Greece.

Imagine this frail child educating himself and then becoming a great orator and leader in Greece. He did not look the part. Statues show him as a frail figure. His brain and voice were his strengths. Demosthenes was courageous and became what many believe to be first lawyer. He fought for the rights of others and promoted Greek culture and freedom. His heart of courage is forever immortalized in statues and his voice is forever recognized as the best in the Ancient world.

Do you feel you lack courage? What are some steps you can take to find your voice and your own courage? Demosthenes stood up to those who stole from him. It was not easy for him to find his courage but he decided and stepped out of his comfort zone. His was a heart of courage.

Questions:

1. What is the most courageous action you ever took?
2. Do you think courage always involves risk? Why or why not?
3. Who is an example of courage to you?

CHAPTER 4

CREATING OPPORTUNITIES

Heart of Moxie
Mary Barra

*"Because I believe with my wholeheartmindbody that girls
constitute a revolutionary soul force that can, and will,
change the world for real."*
- Jennifer Mathieu

*"If you don't have the courage to confront,
you don't have the right to complain.
Don't wait until anger gives you the courage!"*
- Debra Fox

Are men intimidated by strong women? As a father of a daughter, I hope
I have raised my daughter to be strong and determined. Most fathers I
know want the same for their daughters. This is an extremely competitive
world and the workforce is demanding. As a leader, I seek employees
who can communicate and do a job with skill and precision. Whether
you are male or female, you better have the gumption to stand out from
the crowd. You need moxie, or nerve.

I was worried about my daughter as she has tendencies to step back and not stand out. But I have discovered that these are just tendencies. Haley can also be a strong, determined leader with a strong work ethic and the ability to communicate her thoughts and ideas. Haley serves in the Army National Guard in a mostly male-dominated area. She just recently started a job in a field that is dominated by men. Although I am sure she is nervous, she obviously has the ability to handle the pressure she is under or she would not be successful. I am proud of the woman she is becoming and as she develops her skillset, her confidence will grow.

My department's secretary, Johnelle, started experiencing a variety of health issues several years ago. It was as if she was healthy one minute and then suddenly started to fall apart. It became so bad the lights in her office caused her skin to burn as if she was sunburned. When she worked out or even attempted it, her joints would become inflamed and painful. Johnelle went to the doctor for her mysterious symptoms, but he could not figure out what was wrong. Plus, the symptoms changed or would come and go. It took nearly a year and a half for her to finally get a diagnosis.

She was diagnosed with lupus, a chronic, complex autoimmune disease in 2015. She thought she had her answer, but her situation didn't improve. Johnelle went for more tests only to find out that she also has dermatomyositis, a rare autoimmune disease that mimics lupus, only it affects the trunk muscles. This disease also comes with a high risk for malignancy for certain organs. This was obviously not good news for her or her new husband. On top of the diagnosis, she was in a new marriage with a newly blended family.

Johnelle must take nine pills a day and two shots per week. She says, "It is not a pretty picture, some days are good, some days are bad, and some days are spent in the bathroom floor."

Sometimes we receive news, good or bad, that can define us for many years. Johnelle is strong-willed, positive, and determined. With the support of her husband, she has owned her new life and her moxie is evident in how she now lives her life. She kept a new marriage together, took care of children, and attempted to do her job while changing her lifestyle. Her diet has been changed and she must maintain it forever. She constantly works with her doctor to find the right medications for her disease.

It is hard for me to imagine all that Johnelle juggles in her life. Plus, she works in a department full of men and tolerates debilitating pain. I love how she remains positive and demonstrates true moxie in handling it all with grace and humor. She demonstrates we are capable of handling if we set our heart and mind on an objective and remain singularly focused on a desired outcome.

Johnelle has also found something to fight for and that is increased awareness of lupus and dermatomyositis. She attends walks for lupus and goes to seminars and conferences. She hosts a private Facebook group for local women who suffer from autoimmune diseases.

She says, "I try my best to be an inspiration because when I was diagnosed, I was lost. I know how devastated I was and still am."

Still, Johnelle demonstrates true moxie in her life. She wakes up each day determined to keep moving and pressing forward in her life with a strong, determined attitude.

Determination and moxie would define the life of Mary Barra. Many people dream of becoming astronauts, doctors, or professional sport figures. Not Mary. She dreamed of working for General Motors and eventually rose to the rank of Chairman and CEO. She is the first female to lead one of the major automakers in the United States.

Mary grew up in the automotive world. Her father was a die-maker for GM for more than 30 years. She has worked for GM since she was eighteen. She attended the GM Technical school to become an engineer and later graduated from the Stanford Business School. She worked her way up the corporate ladder. During her career, she served as an engineer, plant manager, head of corporate HR, and senior executive overseeing all global and product developments.

Mary's moxie has led her to become the face of General Motors in 2014. Many of the old guard did not expect her to become the head of the company. Yet her predecessor said her promotion was not based on fulfilling a quota or a nod to diversity. It had been earned the hard way. Her determination, extreme hardworking attitude and mindset put her on course to lead the company into the new millennia.

Barra took over GM in the midst of the "Switchgate" scandal, a decadelong cover-up by the company involving faulty vehicle ignition switches installed in several car models. The faulty switches had been connected to the deaths of 12 drivers. Barra's first task as CEO was to take responsibility for the problem and to implement tangible solutions, which included paying reparations to crash victims and their families. She also recalled an initial 1.6 million GM vehicles.

In 2017, Barra was named #1 on the 50 most powerful women in business list in Fortune.

Her moxie is apparent in her drive to get people to embrace change. She is not a motivator, as much as she is driven to be an innovator for moving beyond the gas guzzling vehicles and championing fuel efficient vehicles. Mary is the consummate insider for GM, yet she embraces change and led a company through the government bailout.

When she was hired her first year was devoted to changing safety practices. Several rank and file employees were let go and others were reprimanded. Her leadership style is to lead collaboratively and constructively constantly challenging teams to think, five, ten, and twenty years ahead. Mary's moxie and her fighting spirit keep GM at the forefront of change and innovation. And she knows her product. Mary can often be found at one of test tracks putting a new car through the paces. As a leader, she also knows how to pivot. When auto production slowed during the coronavirus pandemic, Mary teamed with Ventec to use GM's resources to make ventilators for patients.

Embracing her role as the leader of GM while still maintaining a family, Mary does her best to bring normalcy to her life. She has demonstrated that if we live life with passion and work hard we can accomplish our goals and dreams. Mary has found her place in this world and is a true of example of living with a heart of moxie.

Questions:

1. Have you ever had a serious physical condition like Johnelle's, that you had to navigate? How did you do?
2. While Mary Barra is an outstanding example of a successful CEO, why do you think there are so few female CEOs?
3. Was there a time in your life when you had to pivot? When you had to switch directions to survive or get through a trying time.

Heart of Dreams
Marshall "Major" Taylor

"Every great dream begins with a dreamer. Always remember, you have within you the strength, the patience, and the passion to reach for the stars to change the world."
- Harriet Tubman

What dreams do you aspire to come true? What moves your inner spirit to pursue those dreams? I set out five years ago to live my dreams. Now in my late 40's I have had more wonderful things happen to me in the past five years than in the previous 30, with the exception of the birth of my daughter Haley. For example, I used to be terrified of speaking in public. My hands would shake. I would break out in a sweat in front of an audience. But I pushed through that fear to be a speaker today.

I made the decision five years ago to achieve as many of my goals and dreams as I possibly could. In doing so, the only obstacle I have had to face is myself, but others haven't been so lucky. Imagine facing the obstacles of racism, prejudice, abuse, and hatred chasing the dream you love. That was the case with Marshall "Major" Taylor who chased his dream as a world class cyclist in the late 19th century, despite being African American. Marshall Taylor not only chased his dreams, he became the Michael Jordan of his era even though he was often banned from racetracks. White cyclists would team up to block him in and even try to make him wreck.

Cycling in the late 1800s was big business. It was the fastest mode of transportation. The automobile was slow compared to the bicycle. Cycling was big money. Professional cyclists had sponsors and made thousands of dollars, the equivalent to millions in today's money. Cycling could easily fill a stadium with 20,000 to 30,000 spectators. It was bigger than boxing and even matched baseball's popularity.

Cyclist were professionals, gentlemanly, but they raced to win. It could be a very dangerous sport. Many of the races took place on velodromes, short oval tracks shaped like a modern-day NASCAR racetrack, only instead of being flat, they were steeply banked. Cyclists could get up to speeds of 40 mph on these tracks. Imagine racing on heavy metal bikes without helmets and wrecking or being wrecked on purpose? This is what Marshall Taylor endured during his racing career.

Marshall dreamed big even though he experienced racism throughout his career. He started cycling as a delivery boy in Indianapolis but soon start racing. He was mentored by Louis Munger, a bicycle shop owner from the East Coast who entered Marshall in a whites-only race in 1896 in Indianapolis. Marshall couldn't officially compete, yet he set a new world record.

To escape the racism of the Midwest, Marshall moved to Worchester, Massachusetts to work with Munger and help promote his bike shop. This was the hub of American cycling and manufacturing and Munger felt it was a good place to expand his brand. Marshall worked for Munger as a mechanic and ran errands for him.

Munger also encouraged Marshall to race, and race he did. Marshall excelled at the half-mile races and set world records. He also competed in a six-day race at Madison Square Garden where he cycled over 1,730 miles. During these endurance races a cyclist would ride for six days straight 24/7. Cyclist could rest if they chose to do so during these intense endurance races. Those who took breaks and rested fell far behind the pack. Marshall came in 8th and earned the name "The Black Cyclone.".

Marshall traveled the world and dominated cycling for a decade. Even though he endured constant prejudice from his opponents he never stopped chasing his dreams. He was a gentleman and he broke the color barrier by becoming a superstar. He had fans, both black and white, who just wanted to see Marshall "Major" Taylor race and would buy tickets to do so. He had broken seven world records by 1898. In 1899, he raced in the one-mile sprint in Montreal and became only the second black athlete to be a national and international champion in any sport. Despite the racism and prejudice, Marshall became one of the wealthiest athletes of his day.

He was only 32 when he retired from racing, mentally and physically exhausted. Some bad investments and the Great Depression cost him his wealth. With what little money he had left he wrote his autobiography and sold it from his car.

He died penniless and was in a pauper's grave until a group of cyclists in the 1940s moved his body to a more prominent location and erected a bronze plaque in his honor. He has posthumously received numerous accolades including being inducted into the United States Bicycling Hall of Fame in the 1980s. Perhaps what captures Major Taylor best is inscribed on his plaque. "A world champion bicycle racer who came up the hard way without hatred in his heart."

In comparison, it should be easy for us to live with a heart of dreams, yet we sometimes place obstacles in our own path, the biggest one being fear.

Questions:

1. What obstacles are preventing you from living your heart of dreams?
2. Have you ever experienced prejudice? How did you handle it?
3. What do you feel is the most inspiring aspect of Major Taylor's story?

Heart of Daring
Valentina Tereshkova
Sybil Liddington

Be daring, be different, be impractical, be anything that will assert integrity of purpose and imaginative vision against the play-it-safer, the creatures of the commonplace, the slaves of the ordinary." Cecil Beaton

As a young soldier full of myself I would often take the dares of my peers and they would do the same. We were young men growing up and having fun. We dared to seek adventure and test our limits and our will. We relished an opportunity to prove ourselves and our manhood. We dared to be different, which is part of finding yourself as a young adult. While most of us can recall certain times in our lives we were adventurous or bold, those who live with a heart of daring can change the world around them.

Valentina Tereshkova lived in an era where women were considered inferior to men. She also happened to live during the Cold War era, and it was because of the tensions of the times that she forever changed the perception of women.

The United States and Russia were embroiled in a mounting Cold War and the fight for supremacy in space travel. Russia was ahead of the United States in the space race. The Russians launched the first satellite, Sputnik in 1957. On April 12, 1961, Soviet cosmonaut Yuri Alekseyevich Gagarin became the first human being to travel into space aboard the spacecraft Vostok 1. The United States was not far behind as Alan Shepard became the first American in space when the Freedom 7 spacecraft launched on May 5, 1961.

While the Russians were hardly advocates of women's rights, they saw an opportunity to one-up the United States. They decided to send a woman into space. This is when Valentina Tereshkova stepped up and changed the world. She became the first female launched into space on a solo mission on the Vostok 6 on June 16, 1963.

Valentina's daring heart gave her this amazing opportunity. She was born the second of three children to Vladimir and Elena Tereshkova in a small community in western Russia. Her father was killed during World War II when she was only two years old. Her mother was left to raise and support three children by working in the local textile factory.

Valentina's early education suffered and she started school at 10 years old and quit at 17 to work in the textile mill. She started taking correspondence courses. Unbeknownst to her family, she also became interested in parachuting and became a competitive parachutist. This was extremely daring, but it ultimately led to her being chosen to go into space.

Valentina volunteered for the Soviet space program. Although she did not have any experience as a pilot she was accepted because of her parachutist background. She had well over 125 jumps at the time. In the early days of the space program, cosmonauts had to parachute from their capsules seconds before they hit the ground upon returning to earth. Valentina's daring and desire drove her to be a part of something new and uncharted.

Along with four other women, Tereshkova trained to become a cosmonaut for 18 months. The training included tests to determine how she would react to long periods of time being alone, to extreme gravity and zero-gravity conditions. Of the five women, only Valentina was chosen to go into space. Valentina orbited the earth 48 times during a three-day span, all while strapped down in a small, enclosed capsule. In contrast, the four American astronauts who had orbited earth before her had a total of 36 orbits combined. Valentina was hailed as a hero of the Soviet Union.

It would take another 19 years before another Russian woman was launched into space and 20 years before Sally Ride became the first American woman in space. Valentina never flew in space again. She remains the only woman to fly in space solo and the youngest at 26 years old.

Valentina's daring heart led her to become a test pilot and instructor. She also earned her doctorate in technical sciences. The small village girl who started school late is an example that daring to challenge the status quo can change the world. Valentina remains active in the space community and her legacy is celebrated in books, stage productions, and museums throughout the world.

It takes a daring attitude to step out of your comfort zone. It takes looking at yourself in the mirror and seeing beyond that image. The ability to visualize something more is daring from the heart. Valentina's daring actions propelled her to space. Sybil Ludington's heart of daring propelled her and a country to freedom.

Sybil was the female Paul Revere. The difference in Sybil and Paul is that Sybil took her ride alone and rode twice the distance. There are many accounts of Sybil Ludington's ride in the middle of the night April 26, 1777, but none deny the impact.

When I was in boot camp, we had to scale a 40-foot-tower. I was afraid of heights. To scale the tower, we had to interlock hands with our teammates and push and lift each other up the tower. What made this frightening is that we went up the tower on its outside face. If your hands did not lock properly with your teammates, someone could fall to the ground. We climbed four floors, each one more challenging, as we hoisted and lifted ourselves over the edges of the tower all the way to the top. Our teammates pushed us and encouraged us as our four-man teams scaled the tower one floor at a time.

After this daunting challenge, I felt like I could do anything. But it took someone encouraging and literally pushing me to do it. This is how Sybil began her ride with her father encouraging her and telling her she was more than capable of achieving this daring act.

Sybil was the eldest of 12 children by her mother Abigail and father Henry Ludington. Henry had fought in the French and Indian War, and he volunteered to head the local militia during the American Revolution. Sybil was daring even before her ride. She once saved her father from nearly 50 loyalists to the British when they went to Ludington's home to capture Henry. She lit candles all around the house and had her siblings march in front of the windows in military fashion. This created the impression of several troops guarding the house. Upon seeing the silhouettes of the marching children, the Loyalists fled. This daring act could have led to her death and the death of her siblings.

Sybil's daring heart was put to the test on the fateful night in April, although she was only 16. Her father Henry, the militia's colonel, had received word that the British had attacked the town of Danbury and the town needed help. April was prime planting season so the regiment that Henry oversaw had disbanded so each soldier could take care of their respective farms. Someone had to relay the news to them.

While some accounts state that Sybil volunteered, most say that Henry pushed his daughter to ride through the night to gather the troops. Regardless, Sybil was ready. At around 9 p.m., she took off on her horse and in the dark of night rode through the woods in the rain.

Sybil's journey took her through Carmel, New York on to Mahopac, and to Kent Cliffs, and Farmers Mills, before finally returning home. There were few roads during this time, so the journey was tough. Each time her horse wanted to stop and rest, she pressed the horse forward. She traveled nearly 40 miles by the time she was done, a journey that was longer than Paul Revere's infamous ride two years earlier.

By the time she had returned home exhausted, most of the 400 soldiers were ready to march. The Militia arrived too late to save Danbury, but they did drive the British back toward Long Island Sound. Sybil Ludington was congratulated for her heroism by neighbors and friends alike. Probably the most noteworthy recognition came from General George Washington himself. Sybil's heart of daring is a testament to what we can do when we have a dream. In Sybil's case the dream was for a new country and the prospect of freedom.

Live your life with a heart of daring! As a young man and soldier in the Army, I learned to take on challenges that I would not have taken on before. In my later life, I have discovered that I am able to do extraordinary things when I dare to step outside my comfort zone. Valentina demonstrated that by following her passions and living with a heart of daring she could defy the expectations of women at the time. Sybil demonstrated that with a little push, living with a daring heart could help change the course of history.

Be willing to look beyond that face in the mirror. Unleash your dreams and live them fully. Live with a heart of daring.

Questions:

1. Was it easier for you to be daring when you were younger? Why or why not?
2. What do you think is the difference between being daring and foolish?
3. Who do you admire for being daring?

Heart of a Child
Calvin Graham

"Never lose the childlike wonder.
Show gratitude, don't complain; just work harder.
Never give up."
- Randy Pausch

When we were boys, my brother and I often played war like many boys do. Our father was in the army and we wanted to be just like him. But instead of in a foreign land, our wars were fought in the forest behind our houses.

Late one night, my brother and I made torches and left the comfort of our home, torches lit, to meet some friends in an old tunnel to fight a mock midnight war. Once, as a sixth grader living in Colorado, we dressed as barbarian warriors and attacked a family of four walking through a park. We had homemade swords and dressed in homemade loin cloths made of old T-shirts cut in strips and tied around our waist. We basically attacked the family in our underwear.

Screaming and chanting "Attack," we rumbled down the hill toward the family. The children started screaming and I saw a look of both disgust and amusement on the father's face. We immediately ran back in the woods. Once we had regrouped, we all laughed as if we had done something amazing and courageous. We relished the many adventures we shared together.

If you were looking for the Pollard boys, you could always find us in the woods, but you had better be ready to play war. Our childhood dreams drove us to do many foolish things. But our childhood play also helped us to develop into men. The child inside us helped us to dream big dreams.

Children can change the world. They have wonderful imaginations and when left to create and wonder they do amazing creative things. Frank Epperson accidently changed the world with a small stirring stick. On a cold night in the San Francisco Bay Area Frank left a glass of lemon-flavored water with the stick in it on the porch. When he woke the next morning, the concoction had frozen and he licked it clean.

Frank began creating and selling this wonderful cold treat to neighbors and friends. He was 11 years old when he invented the Epsicle. When he got older, his children started calling his Epsicle a Pop's 'sicle and the name stuck. In 1923, he applied for a patent and started selling his popsicles at Neptune Beach, a popular amusement park of the day. Our popular summertime treat and its catchy name were created by children. An accidental winter mistake has helped to cool the tongues of children for over 100 years. Frank had no plans of inventing an Epsicle. He was living with the heart of a child and changed the world.

Calvin Graham dreamed big dreams. He was 11 when he hatched a plan to join the Navy and fight in World War II. Some of his relatives had died in battle and he felt compelled to fight.

At the time, he was one of seven children living in a home with an abusive stepfather. To escape the abuse, Calvin and one of his older brothers moved into a rooming house. He supported himself by delivering telegrams and selling newspapers after school. Imagine going to school and working to support yourself at only 11. But Calvin and his brother were not entirely on their own, as their mother often checked on them to sign report cards and school papers.

As children, we can dream big, but we often have our dreams derailed. Calvin was a child who dreamed big and lived big despite being young and small. He was only about 5'2 and 125 pounds when he started working toward joining the Navy. At the time, the military would take children who were 16 years old with a parent's signature. Calvin was only eleven, but he was not going to wait another five years to enlist.

Calvin started shaving because he thought it would make his beard come in faster. He started talking with a deep voice because he thought it might make him sound older than he was. He and his friends stole a notary stamp in order to forge his parents' signature.

Wearing his older brother's clothes, Calvin showed up at the recruiting station. I can only imagine Calvin standing in line flanked by much larger recruits and the expression on the recruiter's face as he looked up from his paper at the child who stood before him.

But Calvin assured the recruiter he was 17 like his forged paperwork said. Surprisingly, the recruiter let Calvin go through. Although it was common for underage boys, or "baby soldiers" to join the war effort, they were usually closer to 16 than 11 years old. But America was struggling to find able bodied men who could fight. It is estimated that at least 2500 of these baby soldiers fought during World War II.

The recruiter also probably figured that Calvin would not get through the next level of the recruitment process, which was the dental inspection. After all, a dentist can tell how old someone is by looking at their teeth. As the dentist inspected Calvin's teeth he must have wondered how an 11-year-old had managed to make it this far.

The dentist told Calvin to go home, but he refused. Then he played his ace. Calvin had seen the dentist allow a number of underage recruits to go through and he threatened to turn him in if he did not do the same for him. Figuring the kid was not worth the trouble, the dentist allowed him to join the other recruits headed to boot camp.

But what would Calvin tell his parents? He decided to lie and tell them he was going to live with some relatives who lived farther away than his mother could travel. Since a long-distance phone call cost a lot of money, he figured she wouldn't check up on him. His parents agreed to let him go.

Imagine the pint-sized Calvin arriving at boot camp. When I served in the army in 1988, I was an average size recruit. At 12, Calvin must have been the smallest recruit the drill instructors had ever seen.

I remember being scared when I arrived for my first day of boot camp at 17, a recent high school graduate. The drill instructors screamed at each of us new recruits to get off the bus. Then they got in our faces and spit words and obscenities, as we all ran to our assigned areas.

Now I had been a military brat who had traveled the world while my father was in the army. I had been exposed to military life. I was still scared. Calvin had never been outside his small Texas town nor experienced the military. Plus, his drill instructors would have probably treated this baby soldier even harsher just to get him to quit.

Calvin was not a quitter who would give up on his childhood dreams easily. I can imagine the brutal hazing he would have endured from his instructors and other recruits. But he just kept working through boot camp until graduation. I know I was so excited to see my father when I graduated boot camp, but Calvin had to keep his news to himself and just move on to his assigned duty station.

Calvin landed on the USS South Dakota battleship with a crew made up of mostly green soldiers, new recruits who were itching for battle, seeking to avenge the destruction at Pearl Harbor caused by the Japanese. Calvin and his shipmates would get their opportunity in some of the fiercest navy battles of the war at Guadalcanal. The USS South Dakota provided protection to the USS Enterprise aircraft carrier. The South Dakota had a reputation as a ferocious battleship that would even fire on American planes that were low on fuel trying to land on the Enterprise if not properly identified. The ship's captain, Thomas Gatch, was a hardened Navy vet who took personal pride in destroying the enemy.

During the first attack by the enemy, Captain Gatch watched from the bridge as a bomb weighing 500 pounds struck the South Dakota. The explosion injured 50 men, including the captain, whose jugular vein was severed. Quick-thinking crew members helped to save the captain's life.

After repairs at Pearl Harbor, the USS South Dakota was back in business. At the Naval Battle of Guadalcanal, the South Dakota encountered eight Japanese destroyers. Calvin was a gun loader, and despite his diminutive size, he would carry the heavy 40 mm anti-aircraft shells and reload the guns as the ship was under constant attack. Calvin didn't flinch as the ship was struck over 40 times.

As the battle progressed, Calvin was hit by shrapnel and thrown down three flights of stairs. His jaw was damaged and his teeth were knocked out, but Calvin made it to his feet and started helping those who were more injured. He took the belts off the dead men to make tourniquets on the living. With the power out and the ship severely damaged, Calvin provided comfort and aid to the living. He talked to them and brought them cigarettes. He did this throughout the night.

At 13, Calvin was a war hero. He received the Bronze Star and Purple Heart for his actions. Though his age was later revealed by his mother and he was discharged from the Navy, Calvin had experienced more as a 13-year-old then most men do their entire lives. Calvin's heart of a child got him in the Navy. Calvin's heart of service drove him to save his shipmates.

Live with a heart of a child, remind yourself of the dreams you held close in your heart when you were younger. Go after those dreams and goals chase them with all your heart. The only way to make dreams come true is to live each day going after them. Experience life with a heart of a child.

Questions:

1. When you were a child, what was your biggest dream?
2. Can you think of a goal that you pursued as a child or teen without your parent's support or knowledge that makes you proud today?
3. Do you admire Calvin Graham? If so, why?

Heart of Joy
George Foreman

"Find a place inside where there is joy,
and the joy will burn out the pain."
- Joseph Campbell

Finding joy is easy for some but others never seem to find it, like my friend. He has a loving family, a great job, and is relatively successful by middle-class standards. Yet as we have gotten to know one another I realize he is utterly miserable. He hates to go home at night and instead stays out late and shows up after his family has gone to bed. He doesn't like his job and wants to quit. I often ask him why he just does not retire but he just can't seem to bring himself to do it. I have tried to encourage him to get some help, but he is too afraid. When it comes to seeing the joy in his life, he is blind.

In contrast, my father lives in severe pain from his injuries that occurred during the Vietnam War when he was blown off a bulldozer. When he wakes up in the mornings it takes him several minutes to even get out of bed. You would think he would be entitled be miserable. However, he is constantly smiling, laughing, and joking. He is a pleasure to be around even though I can see him grimace or move more slowly at times.

My father lives with a heart of joy. I have always known him to be happy. Even when my parents divorced and he had to work many extra hours to make ends meet, he still put a smile on his face. He still made sure people saw him happy.

How can these two men be so different? The one man who should be joyful is miserable and the man who should be miserable is joyful?

The story of George Foreman's life is one of misery and joy and a life the spanned humble beginnings to boxing royalty to successful entrepreneur. Once George learned to live with joy in his heart he became the smiling lean, mean, grilling machine man we all know and love.

"Big George" Foreman, as he known in boxing circles, was a boxing menace earlier in his career. When he beat Joe Frazier to win the heavyweight championship of the world in 1973 he was 37-0. But Big George said he fought angry during this time.

George grew up in Houston's Fifth Ward, a poor and crime-ridden section of the city. His mother raised him and his six siblings on sometimes $26 a week. He recalled that his mother once brought home a hamburger and cut it up into seven equal portions for the children to share.

George dropped out of school at 15 and joined gangs. He was an admitted thug and extremely angry youth and was anything but joyful. He joined the job corps and met a man that encouraged him to box to release some of his anger. He channeled his anger into boxing and won the 1968 gold medal in the Mexico Olympics. Shortly after the Olympics, he turned professional.

Big George quickly dispatched his opponents. He often pummeled them to submission within the first couple of rounds. George would look at his opponents before each match as if he wanted to destroy them. Old photos and footage depict him as an angry behemoth.

When he knocked out Joe Frazier to win the world championship, he was predicted to lose. Big George fought awkwardly, throwing wide punches. But he still knocked Frazier down six times before the end of the second round scoring a TKO. This should have brought him joy. He should have been happy.

Big George fought Muhammad Ali in what became known as the "Rumble in the Jungle" in 1974. At 32, Ali was considered to be too old and likely to be killed in the ring by the younger Foreman. But Ali did what Ali did best; he got in the head of his opponent. Big George came out throwing his big bombs at Ali. Ali fell against the ropes weaving and bobbing but not absorbing the full force of the blows. George continued to throw his heaviest punches at Ali and by the fifth round was visibly exhausted. As with his previous fights, he expected to knock Ali out within the first couple of rounds.

Near the end of the seventh-round Ali, leaned in toward Big George and whispered, "Is that all you have? I thought you could punch as hard as Joe Louis." Big George knew he was in a different type of fight when he heard Ali speak those words.

In the eighth-round Ali started throwing punches that were easily connecting to his target. With only a few seconds left in the round, Ali dropped Big George to the mat. He had won the world championship in a fight he was not expected to survive. George went into obscurity after his fight with Ali. He only fought a few more times before retiring from boxing.

After his retirement, George became a preacher in his hometown of Houston. He started working with youth and used his winnings from boxing to support himself and youth programs. Big George the fighter had become George the preacher and had finally found his joy.

After ten years of retirement, George wanted to raise some money for his church and his youth programs and decided to return to boxing. He was 38 and the menacing demeanor that had been his trademark when he was younger was gone. He was now fighting for his purpose and his joy. His friendly persona won him new fans and people of all ages fell in love with the man who was older, heavier, and much wiser. He became the oldest heavyweight champion at 45 by knocking out Michael Moore.

George had found his joy and had finally let the anger of his youth disappear. He went on to start his own company selling his now famous George Foreman Grill. And no longer do the burgers have to be split between family members. George is worth an estimated 250 million. He lives with a heart of joy and it has led him to fame and fortune. His joy is in his giving and service to others. When we give, we receive joy.

While my father is not famous or wealthy, he would give the shirt off his back to help a person in need. Like Big George Foreman, his heart is a heart of joy. Live with a heart of joy.

George lived by the credo, "A merry heart will do you the same thing a medicine will do. But a broken spirit will do the same as a knife."

Questions:

1. Have you ever been successful at something, but it didn't make you happy?
2. Big George was able to achieve a boxing comeback. Can you think of a comeback in your life?
3. When do you feel you possess a heart of joy?

CHAPTER 5

STANDING OUT
TAKING CHARGE

Heart of Leadership
Dwight Eisenhower

"The greatest leader is not necessarily the one who does the greatest things. He is the one that gets the people to do the greatest things."
- Ronald Reagan

While serving in Operation Desert Storm, my section chief was Danny Curry. I learned a lot from him. One of the most important things I learned was to take care of your troops. He oversaw us younger soldiers. No one on our six-man team was over 21 years old.

Our lieutenant, or team commander, was Eddie Oliver. He taught us to know our jobs better than anyone else.

Sgt. Curry had joined the army after graduating high school and Lieutenant Oliver had attended West Point, where he played football. Each of them had grown as young leaders themselves and each had a unique style. Sgt. Curry wanted us to be the best team by caring for one another and by putting our team name, D1/41 FIST, over all the other teams. Lt. Oliver wanted us to work harder and be more mission-driven than all the other teams. Together, these two men helped our team consistently outperform the other teams in military drills and training.

When I was first transferred to Sgt. Curry's team I was nervous. My previous section chief did not like me personally and told all the other sergeants I had a bad attitude. I believe it was more that the chief and I just didn't gel.

Upon my transfer, Sgt. Curry did not call me into his office. He came to my barracks room. When he knocked on the door I thought he was there to put me in my place and to tell me that he was the all-powerful section chief who wouldn't tolerate the bad attitude he had heard so much about.

To my surprise none of that happened. Instead he asked me to sit down. Then he politely asked me about my personal life and my expectations of him as my section chief. I was astonished. My previous sergeant, the one with whom I didn't gel, had talked about me negatively without even knowing me. This was an early leadership lesson for me. I learned not to judge others before you get to know them.

After I finished sharing my story, Sgt. Curry declared that I had a fresh start and to go prove them wrong. He invited me into his team, gave me his personal phone number and invited me to his house for dinner. Sgt. Curry cared deeply for his team and wanted only the best for us.

Sgt. Curry was not a weak leader and he had high expectations of his team. If we did not perform up to standards, we would hear about it. He led by being one of us. He never slept in a different tent or wanted us to be subservient to him. He would get in the middle of the dirt and grime with us. If there were opportunities for promotion, we were pushed to prepare for them. As a result, our team wanted to perform at a high standard not just for ourselves, but for him.

Lt. Oliver cared about us as and wanted us to perform at the highest levels as well, but he was mission-oriented. When he was assigned to our team we were all a little leery. We had such a tight knit group, how dare this Lt. Oliver come in and try to take over? Like Sgt. Curry he surprised us, because he did not come in with an ego. Instead, he wanted to learn all he could from each of us. He wanted to be a part of us not for us to be an extension of his ego.

I remember one morning I was performing basic maintenance on our vehicles and he joined me. Lt. Oliver was curious and wanted to know how everything worked to better our mission success. He too was willing to get dirty with us. Lt. Oliver knew when to take direct command of the team and had a knack for asking each of us our opinion without giving up his control.

Sgt. Curry and Lt. Oliver left lasting impressions on me. I have learned that we do not always have to be right to be a good leader. Checking on subordinates is important to the morale of the team. There will be moments when you must take control, but you don't have to do it in a way that hinders the team's overall success.

I have also learned that it is important to remain positive even when things seem bleak and to lead with integrity. If you make a mistake, own it. Do not throw those in your charge to the wolves. What makes a good leader, is a heart of leadership. While I am still a work in progress, these lessons remind me that I must keep working on my weaknesses if I am to be very best leader I can be.

There have been many great leaders in the short history of our country. George Washington was so popular many wanted him to become king of the America's. His strong leadership, however, was guided by principles and integrity. He wanted to see the formation of a free country.

Only a few leaders truly stand out as extraordinary in that they demonstrate four or more quality leadership traits that propel them and those they lead to success, which include being positive, a dynamic, decisive and motivational General Dwight D. Eisenhower possessed more than four of the quality leadership traits. Because of his leadership, the Allied Forces were able to work together and prevail during World War II. He later became president of the United States where he served successfully for two terms.

Dwight grew up in Abilene, Kansas, as the third of seven sons to a poor family. His humble roots would guide him throughout his days of service to the country both militarily and politically. His mother was a devout Mennonite and pacifist, so when he accepted an appointment to attend West Point she was not too happy.

While at West Point, young Ike did not stand out from the crowd. He graduated in the middle of his class in 1915. But what a class! It has gone down in history as the most esteemed class having produced over 59 generals. Despite his talented peers, Eisenhower became the main figure in that group of leaders. This group is nicknamed, "The Class the Stars Fell On." Dwight Eisenhower and Omar Bradley are two standouts from this class who would achieve the rank of five-star general. This is the highest rank a military officer can achieve.

Young Dwight Eisenhower met his wife Mamie while stationed in San Antonio, Texas. The couple married in 1916, and had two sons. One of their sons Doud, died of scarlet fever as a small child. This loss helped to shape Dwight's leadership style of caring for his troops.

Dwight did not serve during WWI, as the war ended just before he was scheduled to go to Europe. Instead, he received an appointment to the Command and General Staff College at Ft. Leavenworth, Kansas. Dwight showed great promise by graduating first in his class of 245 officers. He soon served as military aide to General John J. Pershing, who was commander of the U.S. forces during World War I.

Dwight later served under General Douglas MacArthur, U.S. Army Chief of Staff. During his time serving under MacArthur, he was stationed in the Philippines. Dwight was learning how to deal with strong personalities and how to work with them to better lead. Pershing and MacArthur were powerful Type-A personalities and celebrity figures in the United States.

What we can all learn from Dwight Eisenhower is that few of us are born leaders. Leaders are developed over time and demonstrate a willingness to learn and grow. As Dwight's reputation rose in the Army so did his promotions. He was promoted to brigadier general soon after the outbreak of World War II. George Marshall, who was the Army Chief of Staff, called Eisenhower to Washington, D.C to work as planning officer. Dwight was known for his strategic prowess. He was given command to lead the invasion of North Africa and he later directed the amphibious invasion of Sicily and the Italian mainland that led to the fall of Rome in 1944. After demonstrating numerous successes, in 1943 he was appointed supreme commander of the Allied Expeditionary Forces. It was here that his leadership traits begin to stand out.

Dwight Eisenhower learned to lead over several years of service. He demonstrated many traits of high-achieving leaders as he grew. Having been promoted to full allied commander, he still loved and cared for the troops under his command. He understood that if you are to win battles, it is your teamwork and your care and love for each other, that will pull you through the tough times. He consistently practiced positive optimism.

As allied commander, he had to deal with some dynamic personalities such as Generals George Patton, Omar Bradley, Bernard Montgomery, and let's not forget Winston Churchill. Each of these men brought a different powerful personality to the table. Dwight had to remain optimistic and take responsibility as he balanced these headstrong men.

Though multiple people were planning for the D-Day invasion, Dwight knew that if it failed he would be considered responsible. He owned this fact before the battle ever started. It was this trait that led to General Marshall to appoint him allied commander. He also demonstrated his willingness to take responsibility when he stated: *"Our landings in the Cherbourg-Havre area have failed to gain a satisfactory foothold, and I have withdrawn the troops. My decision to attack now was based upon the best information available. The troops, the air, and the Navy did all that bravery and devotion to duty could do. If any blame or fault attaches to the attempt, it is mine alone."*

Of all the leadership traits that Dwight displayed the most important was his integrity. He once stated, "The supreme quality for leadership is unquestionably integrity. Without it, no real success is possible, no matter whether it is on a section gang, a football field, in an army, or in an office." His integrity shone brightly during World War II, when he took a cruise around the Isle of Capri. On seeing a large villa, he asked about it and learned it would be his headquarters. He then noticed another large villa, and learned that it would belong to his Army Air Force General Carl Spaatz. Eisenhower was livid.

He said, "Damn it, that is not my villa and that's not General Spaatz's villa!" He told his commanders this was not to be a playground for the top brass. He never set himself apart from his soldiers. His humble beginnings in Kansas had helped mold his leadership style. Commanders such as MacArthur were elitist generals who put themselves on pedestals. Not Eisenhower. Even though he was the Allies' leading commander, he still saw himself as a soldier's generals.

Dwight Eisenhower earned his fifth star during the war because he proved to be diligent, effective, and a strategic thinker. He believed that leadership did not come from demanding or barking orders or mandating action. He said, "You do not lead by hitting people over the head. That's assault, not leadership." He believed leadership was not about pushing your ideas. Leadership is about respectful conversation and listening from both sides.

General Eisenhower demonstrated patience in dealing with his counterparts. He said of the war, "In a war such as this, when high command invariably involves a president, a prime minister, six chiefs of staff, and a horde of lesser planners, there has got to be a lot of patience--no one person can be a Napoleon or a Caesar." He understood the value of patience and that the coalition of military and world leaders were necessary to accomplish the mission.

In reflecting on his leadership style, "I adopted a policy of circulating through the whole force to the full limit imposed by my physical considerations. I did my best to meet everyone from the general to private with a smile, a pat on the back and definite interest in his problems."

General Eisenhower did not boost morale with speeches, but with simple, honest conversations. After the war this guided him in his presidency. He led the country during the tumultuous beginnings of the Cold War, remaining optimistic about the country's future. He promoted the building of the interstate system. His only perceived setback was how he handled civil rights. Yet he did promote judges to the bench who were favorable to those issues. Over his lifetime, President Eisenhower grew as a leader and led with a heart of leadership.

As I have gotten older, I have looked to those leaders who have influenced me the most. My dad has had the most profound effect on me. He loved his soldiers and his family but he was tough and expected hard work. Sgt. Curry taught me to put the team first and to care for the members of the team. This led to our cohesive, strong bond before, during, and after the war.

Lt. Oliver taught me to be meticulous when planning and preparing for a mission and to know my job as best I could. I know there are things I can work on, patience being one of them. I am working on it, though, and recognizing this as an area of weakness.

I do care deeply for my subordinates and I desire only their success. If they succeed, I succeed. Their opinions and ideas and thoughts are valuable when we are tasked with a mission. I have been blessed with a myriad of personalities to work with. They each bring a unique perspective to our department and help us to perform at the highest level.

I am sure Dwight Eisenhower felt the same way about his soldiers. Go out and learn to grow as a leader and develop and hone your leadership skills. This will help you become a leader that leads from the heart.

Questions:

1.   Who do you consider to be a great leader?
2.   What are the important qualities of a leader?
3.   Do you consider yourself a leader?

Heart of Dedication
Barbara Jordan | Daniel Hale Williams

"If you believe in yourself and have dedication and pride and never quit, you'll be a winner. The price of victory is high but so are the rewards."
- Paul "Bear" Bryant

My mother and father taught us children to be dedicated to our causes. As a student who struggled through school, it was hard to be dedicated to my education. I did not realize at the time what an education truly meant to my future. Only after I joined the Army and had served in Operation Desert Storm did I truly realize that I needed to be dedicated to my own success or failure. I understood that without an education life was going to be much tougher for me.

When I finally decided to become a teacher during Desert Storm, it was at the lowest point of my life, having witnessed death and destruction. I realized I had something to offer others. I just needed to find a way to get there, so I dedicated myself to pursuing an education.

Education has been a springboard for many people, particularly those from disadvantaged backgrounds. Barbara Jordan and Dr. Daniel Hale Williams used education to catapult them from their humble beginnings and their heart of dedication changed and saved lives throughout America.

Barbara Jordan was born to a Baptist minister in one of the poorest neighborhoods in Houston. Early on, she had a drive to do more with her life. Her parents encouraged her to pursue her education as her path to escape her surroundings. Barbara excelled at school and was gifted with language and her ability to build and win arguments. In high school she was an award-winning debater and orator. She graduated from Texas Southern University in 1956 and attended Boston University Law School. She was a minority, only one of only a handful of black students, and a female at that.

The nation was gripped by social change in the form of major civil rights issues during that time. Barbara found her calling and became dedicated to defending the constitution.

Upon graduating from law school, she moved back to Texas and opened a practice in her parents' home. This is where she became interested in politics seeing the daily lives of her neighbors and the injustices they suffered. She became a campaigner for John F. Kennedy and Lyndon Johnson. She ran unsuccessfully for the Texas Legislature twice before she made history in 1966 by being elected the first black woman to win a seat.

When she arrived in Austin, she was not greeted with open arms by the other legislators. Eventually, her dedication to the law and the constitution began to win some of her colleagues over. While serving in the Texas Legislature she fought for Texas Fair Employment Practices and sponsored or cosponsored some 70 bills. In 1972, she again made news by becoming the first African American woman to be president pro tempore of the state senate.

As a rising political star in Texas, she decided to run for the U.S House of Representatives for her district. She won the election in 1972 and was off to Washington D.C. She became a member of the House Judiciary Committee, where she was put in the spotlight during the Watergate scandal.

A powerful and gifted orator, Barbara is most famous for her role during the Watergate hearings. During the nationally televised impeachment she famously stated, "I am not going to sit here and be an idle spectator to the diminution, the subversion, the destruction of the Constitution." Barbara was dedicated to the constitution of the United States and was not about to see this living document fail during this time.

In 1976, she was mentioned as a possible running mate to Jimmy Carter. Instead, she became the first African American woman to deliver the keynote address at the Democratic National Convention. She told the crowd, "My presence here is one additional bit of evidence that the American dream need not forever be deferred."

She had hoped to be chosen as Carter's attorney general, but he selected someone else. No matter Barbara Jordan was dedicated to the letter of the land and service to others. She decided not to run for reelection to her house seat in 1978 and it was later revealed that she had been diagnosed with multiple sclerosis.

Barbara decided to dedicate her life to the next generation of politicians and public officials. She became a professor at the University of Texas at Austin, leading future generations to take up the cause of dedication to the constitution and public service.

In 1994, President Bill Clinton awarded her with the presidential Medal of Freedom for her service to the United States. Barbara Jordan never allowed herself to be defined by her community or the poor economic conditions she was born into. She lived a life dedicated to a cause that helped all citizens not just African Americans. She stood strong in an era defined by civil rights issues and changing times. Barbara lived with a heart of dedication.

When we find our causes or reasons to live they come completely without question from the heart. Daniel Hale Williams found his passion and dedication from an actual heart. He was one of the first surgeons to perform open heart surgery in the United States. The fact that he performed open heart surgery was remarkable for the mid-1890's. What made this achievement more remarkable is that he was black.

Daniel came from modest circumstances much like Barbara Jordan. He was born in 1856 in Pennsylvania. His parents, Daniel Williams II and Sarah Williams, were poor and under the conditions of the day probably watched their movements closely so as not to draw attention from the white population. Although Pennsylvania was a free state, black Americans were not necessarily free.

Daniel's father was a barber and after the Civil War he worked with the equal rights league, a black civil rights organization active during Reconstruction. He was only ten when his father died, and he was sent to live with family friends in Baltimore.

While living in Baltimore, he became a shoemaker's apprentice. Daniel disliked the work and moved back to his family who had made their way to Illinois. He followed in his father's footsteps and took up barbering, but then decided to pursue his education. He started working as an apprentice with Dr. Henry Palmer, a highly accomplished surgeon. As he worked with Dr. Palmer, Daniel found his calling. He attended and trained at the Chicago Medical College.

When Daniel graduated, he set up a practice in Chicago's South Side and taught anatomy at his alma mater. This was a remarkable achievement for an African American during the 1800s. There were not many black surgeons during this time, even though they were growing in numbers. Daniel became the first African American physician to work for the city street railway system. All his patients affectionately called him Dr. Dan. Because of the discrimination of the day, African Americans were barred from being admitted to hospitals and black doctors were refused staff positions.

Dr. Dan's dedication to medicine and equal rights were spurred on by the discrimination he had to endure. He decided to open his own hospital named Provident Hospital and Training School for Nurses in 1891. This was the nation's first hospital with a nursing intern program that had a racially integrated staff. The facility where he worked as a surgeon was publicly championed by famed abolitionist and writer Frederick Douglas.

Dr. Dan was most famous for the surgery he performed in 1893. He made history when he operated on James Cornish, a man with a severe stab wound to his chest who had been brought to Provident Hospital. Without the benefits of blood transfusion or modern surgical procedures, he successfully sutured Cornish's pericardium, the membranous sac enclosing the heart. This act made him the first person to successfully perform open heart surgery.

Imagine the bravery and dedication it must have taken to even think of performing such a surgery. By all accounts Cornish made a full recovery and lived many more years thanks to Dr. Dan's surgical skill and dedication to his patients. Dr. Dan was driven by his dedication to medicine, and racial equality. These drove him to success at all levels of his life.

Dr. David Hale Williams passed in August 1931, five years after suffering a stroke. He has never been forgotten and to this day his work as a pioneering physician and advocate for an African American presence in medicine continues to be honored worldwide. From humble beginnings, Daniel grew from shoemaker's apprentice to barber to esteemed physician who opened an integrated hospital.

Barbara Jordan and Dr. Daniel Hale Williams are proof of the American dream. They both achieved many firsts in their respective careers. Their firsts were driven by the heart of dedication that drove both to work hard and perform at the highest levels. When we are dedicated to our goals, passions, and dreams, and refuse to be held back by our surroundings, we can be capable of miraculous things.

Questions:

1. Do you think it is harder to achieve when you come from a modest background?
2. What are you are most dedicated to?
3. Do you have be dedicated to be successful? Is yes, why?

Heart of Enthusiasm
Steve Irwin

"Enthusiasm releases the drive to carry you over
obstacles and adds significance to all you do."
- Norman Vincent Peale

The hard thud of someone banging on the door to my barracks room while stationed in Germany became a regular thing during my military service in the Army. My friend John would bang on the door and bellow, "Let's go do some PT hoorah!" John's enthusiasm was welcome to all of us forward observers who lived in the woods playing army. When we were not in the woods we lived in the barracks and did regular army infantry training. Shoot, move, and communicate was our credo. John made the monotony of it fun and enjoyable.

John's pure enthusiasm made cold, rainy, miserable days bearable. He was full of joy and remained motivated all the time. If he was having a bad day, he would simply smile and make some comment to the effect that this too will soon pass. If John saw that a fellow soldier was discouraged he would run up to them smile and blurt out some silly army saying. Soon, the solider was smiling along with John. When us young soldiers complained about having to clean or shine our boots, John would find a way to make a competition out it.

One time, John volunteered me and our friend Michael to compete in a ruck march competition. A ruck march is done by wearing full battle gear weighing in excess of 65 pounds not including our weapons. The march was around 10 miles and made up of three member teams. Mike and I were not as enthusiastic as John was especially since he volunteered us for the competition on one of our few Saturdays off. When we protested, he said it was for a good cause. The money raised went to help foster kids.

As soon as the competition began all three of us took off. John kept encouraging us and remained enthusiastic throughout the event. The gear was heavy and the terrain was rough but John made it fun and encouraged us all the way. As we passed the finish line in second place, we all embraced in a group man hug. John bought us beer that night and we laughed about the event and how we each fell a few times and how a group of older soldiers/the old team? passed us right at the end.

John and I have remained friends for nearly 30 years. If I need a laugh or a little motivation, I call John. His enthusiasm helped us while stationed in Germany and in Desert Storm, and I know it has helped the people he supervises at work every day. John lives with a heart of enthusiasm in everything he does. When we approach our lives and our current situations enthusiastically, we might just be able to brighten the day of someone in need.

Steve Irwin lived his life with extreme enthusiasm. The colorful TV personality and wildlife expert enthralled his audiences through his show The Crocodile Hunter. His charisma and energy helped his show thrive from 1992 to 2006, the year he died. His passion and enthusiasm now live on in reruns and through his family.

Steve's enthusiastic spirit and love of animals were in his blood. When he was only eight years old his parents moved to Queensland, Australia where they purchased four acres of land and opened a small wildlife park. Steve's father, Ben, described him as a monster growing up. His mother Lyn, was a bit nicer and described him as hyperactive. She recalled that from the time he was two years old he was climbing trees and running off to play in the woods. Steve was born enthusiastically adventurous.

Steve's enthusiasm helped to grow his parent's wildlife park, Beerwah, into a major tourist attraction, which later became known as the Australia Zoo. His career started because he started videotaping some of his animal exploits and shared the videos with a producer. The producer did a ten-hour documentary and called it The Crocodile Hunter. It was so well-received it led to another one and made Steve a star. He became known as the best crocodile hunter in all of Australia.

His success enabled him to grow the zoo from what started on only four acres of land to an over 60-acre attraction. Today, the Australia Zoo employees over 360 people and has over 1000 animals.

Steve is most familiar to Americans from his hit television show based on the documentary, *The Crocodile Hunter*, which helped him and his family promote animal conservation throughout the world. During one of his many interviews, he was asked to describe his infectious excitement and enthusiasm. Steve stated, "I believe that education is all about being excited about something.…That's the main aim in our entire lives is to promote education about wildlife and wilderness areas, save habitats, save endangered species, etc. So, if we can get people excited about animals, then by crikey, it makes it a heck of a lot easier to save them."

Although Steve's enthusiastic nature was well-received throughout the world, to some in his home country of Australia he was a shameless self-promoter. They felt he made all Australians look like the character from Crocodile Dundee. Others saw Steve as just another friendly bloke from the outback. No matter what the public thought of him, Steve never wavered in his enthusiasm for animal conservation. At the height of his career, he was the most recognizable figure in Australia.

Sadly, Steve passed in 2006 after being stung by a stingray while on location for a documentary entitled, ironically, *Ocean's Deadliest*. He was doing what he loved most, promoting animal rights and conservation. Even though many animal rights activists did not always like his methods and how he handled animals, none of them can deny his influence on promoting conservation. Because of his hit television show, many children went on to work in conservation and became zoologists. His own children, Bindi and Robert, followed him into the business as conservationists and celebrities, with successful TV shows of their own.

Steve's passion and pure unadulterated enthusiasm inspired others to care about animal rights and conservation. For others, he offered educational entertainment. Steve Irwin lived with a heart of enthusiasm. We should all find ways to live with the same enthusiasm that he did.

Questions:

1. 1, What are you enthusiastic about?
2. Are passion and enthusiasm one in the same? Why or why not?
3. Do you feel that Steve Irwin is an admirable figure? Explain.

Heart of a Peacemaker
Elisabeth Vincken

When my brother and I were kids we fought like kids do, arguing, fighting one another and then making up when it was all done. My mother often intervened and would make us hug and make up. We did a lot of hugging.

I was the neat freak; my little brother the messy one. If he played with my toys and did not return them to their proper place I was mad. If I messed with his stuff or teased him he was mad. My brother and I fought a lot but we loved one another.

When I went to Desert Storm I was trained to loathe my enemy and fight to kill him. I am sure my enemy was trained to do the same thing. As adults, we are not often very forgiving and at times can hold grudges that go on for years. If we are lucky, we find a peacemaker who intervenes and helps us forget why we are even angry. But that wasn't the case in Desert Storm.

When the hostilities of Desert Storm subsided, it was because we had won the battles necessary to stop the war, not because we did anything to promote peace. I cannot imagine me wanting anything to do with my enemy while we were embroiled in fighting. I had friends who were killed during the war and I hated my enemy and was angry for many years afterward. While my mom was the peacemaker when I was a child, there was no circumstance that had opened the window to peace during the actual fighting. What if I had been given an opportunity to sit down with my enemy? What if a peacemaker had appeared and opened the dialogue even for a brief moment? I may not have spent years angry because of the war.

Sometimes unpleasant events can open the doors to peace. My mother spent years struggling with anger and often took it out on my brother and me. We believe she was dealing with depression that had been dormant for years, but would rear its ugly head periodically. I would not speak with her sometimes for days because I did not want to deal with a hateful comment that would invariably come out of her mouth. Her comments could sting, and I took them personally. Yet my mother was wonderful when she was calm, and her mind seemed at peace.

Holidays could be hard for my family. After my parents divorced, my mother often started a fight or family drama right before the holidays. This made holiday gatherings stressful and joyless until she left. It took an event to change all this for my family. The event was my mother realizing that she needed to change and get some help.

My brother was closer to my mother than I was and could reason with her and talk to her. One day late in September my mother and I had been arguing. My brother always seemed to intervene to smooth things over, but he had finally had enough and told my mother she needed to get help and go to counseling or she was going to lose her family.

My mother took this threat seriously. She started counseling and started to work to finally resolve the issues she had.

Christmas of 2015 was and still is one of the best we have ever had. My mother did not cause any drama; she was loving and caring. The family played games, we laughed, and we celebrated the holiday with joy, love, and care for each other. Little did we know that three days later, our mother would be dead.

I am forever grateful for my brother intervening with our mother and being a peacemaker. I am forever grateful to my mother for finding peace that final Christmas together. Sometimes an event can change our perceptions, our beliefs, and how we feel about others. Christmas 2015 was that unforgettable event for our family.

Elisabeth Vincken was a peacemaker. She was mother of a young son and lived in Germany during World War II..

It was Christmas Eve 1944. The weather was brutally cold. The Americans and Germans were in the midst of some of the fiercest fighting of the World War II, the Battle of the Bulge. The Germans had put together one of their last offensive onslaughts of the war. This battle was their last hope to push the Allies back and have any hope of winning the war.

Elisabeth and her young son had been taken to the Ardennes Forest to wait out the war after being bombed in their home in Aachen, Germany. They had made it to the small hunting cabin and thought it was a safe place to hide for the remainder of the war. Her husband was a soldier and was hoping to make it home for the holidays, but had not arrived.

Elisabeth and her son Fritz had very little food, a few potatoes and a small rooster she had affectionately named Hermann Goering, the Nazi Leader in charge of creating the concentration camps or death camps. It was fitting, as Elisabeth didn't like Goering and Hermann the rooster would be their dinner for the holidays.

As they tried to stay warm in the small cabin using candles and a small fire they heard a knock at the door. Elisabeth opened the door to see two American soldiers with their guns standing in front of her and one laying in the snow. Elisabeth and Fritz were scared, but she invited the soldiers in, particularly when she noticed one of them had been shot and was severely injured.

Elisabeth had Fritz go get six small potatoes and prepare Hermann to be a meal for everyone. She then tried to help the injured soldier with his injuries. Neither side spoke the other's language, but Elisabeth and one of the Americans both knew some French and were able to communicate a little. As the soldiers rested there was another knock at the door. Fritz, believing it was more Americans, quickly opened the door. Standing at the door were four German soldiers.

Elisabeth knew that the penalty for harboring the enemy was execution. She must have been extremely frightened with three American soldiers inside her small cabin staying warm, and four German soldiers, weapons drawn, standing at the door. All the soldiers had endured some fierce fighting and most certainly had lost friends and fellow soldiers. Each of them probably felt animosity toward the other because of the fighting.

Elisabeth thought quickly and invited the Germans in, but warned them they would not be happy with what they saw inside. The corporal asked if it was Americans and Elisabeth explained that like them, the Americans had lost their way in the dark and stumbled across her cabin. Elisabeth then summoned her courage and told the soldiers no shooting or fighting would take place this holy night. She told the soldiers to set their weapons outside by the door and invited the German soldiers in to warm their weary bodies. She then grabbed the American's guns and set them outside the cabin with the Germans' weapons.

The tension in the small cabin must have been unbearable. Two enemies, a young German lady and her twelve-year-old son in close quarters. After a few minutes the smell of Hermann and the potatoes cooking helped to ease the tensions in the room. A German soldier pulled out a loaf of bread and a bottle of wine. Each group began to calm down and tensions relaxed. Another German soldier had been a medical student before the war and began to help the injured American soldier. He explained that the snow and cold weather had probably actually helped his wounded leg from becoming infected.

When Hermann and the potatoes were ready to be eaten, Elisabeth gathered all the soldiers together, closed her eyes and began to pray. She prayed for the war to be over and for peace. As she opened her eyes, she saw that all the soldiers had tears in their eyes. She realized these soldiers were just boys. The Americans could not have been more than 20 years old and at least two of the German soldiers were not more than 16.

For the remainder of the night the soldiers played games and rested. When they all woke in the morning the Germans helped the Americans by pointing them in the direction of the Allied Forces. They each thanked Elisabeth and Fritz and went their separate ways.

Elisabeth's motherly act as peacemaker one Christmas night long ago helped to change the perception one enemy had toward another. For one night, in her small cabin, this young mother proved that peace can be achieved in the harshest of times if someone is strong enough to have the heart of a peacemaker.

Questions:

1. In what situations, have you been forced to be a peacemaker?
2. Have you ever had to make peace while struggling with fear? What was the situation?
3. Have you ever had to deal with an enemy and came to understand them a little better?

Heart of a Warrior
Master Sergeant Woodrow Keeble

"Don't be afraid of anything,
be braver than that which scares you the most."
- Wowaditaka

I love warriors and their stories of valor and heroism and the story of Woodrow Wilson Keeble is an inspiration to me. Woody, as he was called by peers, family and friends epitomized the heart of a warrior, particularly in battle. He was not scared and was awarded the medal of honor posthumously for his feats of valor. Although he lived in pain toward the end of his life, he was a warrior to the very end.

Woody, a Sioux Indian, joined the army to fight in World War II even though he had just been drafted by the Chicago White Sox to play baseball. But as a Sioux Indian, he had to go fight for his country to live out his warrior creed. Standing at over six feet and weighing nearly 230 pounds, Woody towered over other men of his era. But for his size, he was surprisingly nimble and quick. His peers grew to love and admire him quickly because of his personality and leadership skills. As soon as his soldiers realized how brave he was, they looked to him to lead the charge.

Woody's first acts of heroism took place during the battle of Guadalcanal, which involved some of the fiercest hand-to-hand combat of World War II. During this battle, Woody distinguished himself as one of the bravest soldiers in his unit. His peers told stories of Woody going ahead of the unit to take out snipers and enemy patrols before they arrived.

As a warrior, Woody chose to protect his peers at all cost. He did not just go ahead of the unit to kill the enemy. Woody went to the front to protect his men at his own peril, and later received the first of his four purple hearts and the bronze star for valor while serving in WWII.

After WWII, Woody returned to the reservation where he taught school and coached youth sports and became an advocate for veterans. He loved protecting these former soldiers and working with them as he had done during the war. Woody wore his old uniform as a badge of honor and a symbol of the pride he felt for his service to his country, while serving others in his tribe.

When the Korean War began, Woody enlisted, even though his friends told him he had nothing to prove and had already served with valor in a war. But he was undeterred and explained to his peers that he knew how to fight in war and felt compelled to help those who had not. Again, his warrior spirit stood out as he went to Korea to fight.

Despite his heroic feats and exemplary service in World War II, Woody faced his biggest challenges in Korea. During a fierce battle, most of the leadership within his unit had been injured or killed. Only Woody, now a master sergeant, and one low-ranking officer were left to lead three platoons up a highly fortified hill that needed to be secured. There were trenches filled with enemy soldiers, three pillboxes containing machine guns and additional men surrounding the hill.

Woody led the three platoons in successive assaults upon the Chinese who held the hill throughout the day. All three charges were repulsed, and Woody's company suffered heavy casualties.

But Woody wanted to try one more time. Armed with grenades and his automatic rifle, he crawled to an area 50 yards from the ridgeline, flanked the left pillbox and, using grenades and rifle fire, eliminated it. After returning to the point where 1st Platoon held the company's first line of defense, Keeble worked his way to the opposite side of the ridgeline and took out the right pillbox with grenades. As if this was not enough, Woody worked his way toward the middle pillbox. He then lobbed a grenade into the back entrance of the box and concentrated fire on the pillbox. As Woody worked his way toward the third pillbox, the enemy concentrated all their fire in his direction.

One witness said there were so many grenades thrown toward Woody that it looked like a flock of blackbirds. Still, Woody would not order his men to advance until all three pillboxes were taken out. Despite serious injuries that soaked his uniform with blood, he refused to leave the battlefield until he knew the three platoons were safe.

Only then did he allow himself to leave the field of battle for medical attention. Woody's wounds were numerous, with wounds in his chest, both arms, right calf, right knee, right thigh and left thigh. In all, he had over 83 grenade fragments removed from his body.

After the war, Woody returned to the reservation, but he was not the man he had been when he left. He lived in constant pain, and even walking was an effort. He developed tuberculosis and would ultimately die from the disease. However, Woody, ever the warrior, continued to support and help veterans. He would visit the veterans home wearing his uniform and tell stories and play games. He would ride in parades wearing his uniform. He was a proud warrior.

Woody was recommended for the Medal of Honor twice for his valor and both times the paperwork was lost. In fact, he did not receive this honor until 26 years after his death. But medals did not drive him. As a warrior, he was driven by the fight and he served and protected veterans all his life, ever displaying the Heart of a Warrior.

As a veteran myself, Woody's devotion and sacrifice to his unit and to other soldiers long after his service was over motivates me to take that warrior spirit into my everyday life.

Questions:

1. Do you consider yourself a warrior?
2. How do you display the heart of a warrior in your everyday life?
3. Who would you protect at all costs?

CHAPTER 6

EMBRACING YOUR CHOICES

Heart of Play
The Tarahumara Indians

"Do you know what my favorite part of the game is?
The opportunity to play."
- Mike Singleton

As a child of the 1970s, I played outside until mother made us come in. My friends and I built tree houses, created little gangs, and ran through the woods playing army. Everything we engaged in was related to play. As adults, we seem to lose that heart of play.

The Tarahumara Indians of Chihuahua, Mexico live their lives with a heart of play. They are renowned for their running ability. Living high in the Copper Canyon mountains, they have been known to run 200 to 300 miles at a time. They do this for inter-village communication, transportation, and hunting. The Tarahumara or Raramuri (runners on foot or those who run fast) have been known to run down their prey until the animals die from exhaustion.

Although it is part of their culture to run to hunt and communicate, the Tarahumara are extraordinary in that they do it for the pure joy or for play. The Tarahumara children and adults play games while they run.

The boys will kick a wooden ball from one relay to another sometimes for several hours or days at a time. The girls will twirl a hoop on a stick as they run from one relay point to the next. Running is an event of play for the Tarahumara. They do not think in terms of winning and losing, they think only in terms of play.

For a short period, the Tarahumara entered professional long-distance racing, including the famed Leadville race in Colorado. They had a sponsor who gave them brand new shoes and all the latest equipment designed for running. As the Tarahumara ran the course with the issued gear, they became uncomfortable. After several miles, these Indians threw off all their expensive gear and put on their usual running shoes, sandals made from old tires and twine. The Tarahumara came in first, second, and fourth. The winner was in his fifties. The other competitors were in awe of this strange group of men who seemed to get stronger as the race went along, who seemed to glide along one hundred miles of some of the toughest terrain at the highest elevations.

For a time, the Tarahumara had sponsors and won many long distances races. What was once play for those competitive racers changed to corporate greed for sponsors and those who once raced for the joy of running lost something. They lost their heart of play.

When we lose our sense of play, we allow what others may think to affect our decisions and goals. We forget that we have our own dreams and desires that may or may not align with our world.

When I was raising Haley, I was solely devoted to my daughter. That is what we do as parents; you put your children first. And while raising Haley, I got to play. We wrestled, played with toys and dolls, watched Disney movies and went on many adventures. Haley and I chased armadillos, kept crickets, caught bugs, performed scientific experiments, and even played sports. I spent my life raising Haley with a heart of play.

When Haley graduated high school and left for boot camp however, I was heartbroken, and it took me some time to figure out a plan for myself. I realized I had not lived for my own play and pleasure. My plan was to start doing the things I had wanted to do all along. I started working out harder and longer and entering obstacle course races. I began listening to audiobooks and reading more. I started living for me and my own playtime. My heart is still devoted to my daughter and my wife. I have just learned to balance what brings me joy and a sense of play with what does the same for them.

I want to live like the Tarahumara Indians, who run with a Heart of Play. Play that is untethered and part of all that I am and hope to become, just like the children of the Tarahumara who are raised not to compete, but to participate with a Heart of Play.

Questions:

1. Do you think losing your Heart of Play is just a casualty of growing up?
2. When was the last time you possessed a Heart of Play?
3. What were you doing when you felt that way?

Heart of Loyalty
Hachiko

"Nothing is more noble, nothing more venerable, than loyalty."
- Cicero

We recently had to put down our beloved family dog, Clem. He was over fifteen years old and suffered from extreme kidney disease. Clem was originally not my dog. He belonged to my wife when we started dating. But when we married, and with the passage of time, Clem became my dog just as much as hers. When I would get home from work he would follow me around the house. When I went to bed, he would often come into the room with me. While I would joke how much I disliked him, I was heartbroken when we had to put him to sleep.

Clem was loyal to the very end. Even as he was sick and suffering he would try to hold his head up and lick us in his friendly way. That silly old beagle mix got to me. Clem demonstrated true loyalty.

I am loyal to those I fought in the war with, my wife, daughter, and father. I am loyal to those I work with and supervise and would help in any way I can. But how much has my loyalty been tested? And if the answer is not much, is this true loyalty?

Hachiko demonstrated true loyalty until his death. He was the beloved pet of Hidesaburo Ueno, an agricultural professor at the Tokyo Imperial University in the 1920s. Hachiko was an Akita, a very large breed of dogs normally used on farms. However, because cities were beginning to thrive throughout Japan, the Akita breed had dwindled in popularity until there were only about 30 purebred Akitas left in the country.

Ueno adopted Hachiko from a farm and brought him home to Tokyo, a young thriving city with nearly eight million inhabitants. Each day the professor would commute on the train to work. Each day Hachiko would leave his home and go to the train station to wait on Ueno to come home.

One day Ueno suffered a cerebral hemorrhage and passed away while giving a lecture. That day, Hachiko went to meet him at the station as usual. And for the next eight years, the dog went to the train station daily to wait for his owner Ueno to return.

Hachiko must have been a scary sight waiting alone unleashed. Male Akitas can weigh up to 130 pounds. He may have been scared himself and may have experienced abuse at the train station, kicks or taunts. Still, every day he showed up to wait on Ueno.

Ueno would never return, but Hachiko and his loyalty were finally recognized in a series of articles written by one of Ueno's former students. Once word of Hachiko's loyalty spread he became famous. Many of the commuters and local store owners would greet and welcome him. His loyalty was used by the government to promote allegiance toward the emperor and the military.

Hachiko passed away in 1935 but the dog was not forgotten. A permanent statue was erected at the Shibuya Station in 1948, which still stands and is a popular meeting post. Books have been written about him. A movie inspired by Hachiko, "Hachi: A Dog's Tale," featuring Richard Gere was released in 2009. His loyalty has inspired generations.

When times are tough and you have been kicked around for staying loyal to your cause, it may seem useless to persist. People may reject you and your efforts may seem hopeless. Stay the course. Remain loyal to yourself and your beliefs. Hachiko suffered many long years without Ueno, but near the end, his efforts were recognized by an entire country. He inspired many and he was rewarded with love and affection until his passing and is remembered today for his loyalty. Hachiko demonstrated true loyalty to the very end.

Questions:

1. Do you consider yourself a loyal person? Why?
2. Can you think of a story of loyalty that inspired you?
3. Where does loyalty rank on your list of qualities you admire in others?

Heart of Confidence
Jack Johnson

"Always be yourself--express yourself, have faith in yourself.
Do not go out and look for a successful personality and duplicate it."
- Bruce Lee

I went through a period where I lacked confidence. It showed up mostly around my peers. My anxiety did not show when I spoke to students. I could have spoken to an auditorium full of students with confidence.

But when it came to talking to faculty members and staff in a large forum or setting I was visibly shaken. I would sweat so bad that my forehead would drip with perspiration. My clean pressed dress shirts would be soaked with sweat. Most of all, I would start shaking uncontrollably.

I think my loss of confidence started when I moved from being an assistant principal at an elementary school to an assistant principal at a high school. Even though I had worked with high school students in the past, I felt inferior to the staff of teachers and administrators.

I started attending school board meetings and meetings with city officials and others, which were not required of my role as an assistant principal, but helped me gain more confidence. It took me nearly two and half years to become comfortable working with the staff at the high school level before my nervousness and anxiety dissipated. Once I overcame this flaw in myself I felt stronger and was soon offered my own school as a principal. My confidence had returned and it was noticeable in my health, the school, the community, and my own family. But for some, their confidence never wavers.

Jack Johnson grew up in Galveston, Texas to former slaves. His parents struggled to make ends meet. They saved what they could and bought a small home for the family and made sure Jack and all his siblings were educated and could read and write. Jack became an avid reader and played the bass violin. And even as a young man he had confidence. He knew he would be well known for something, he just didn't know it would be for boxing.

It was the Jim Crow Era where racial segregation was enforced. But despite overt racism, Jack determined he was not going to live his life as a second-class citizen. This took confidence. White boxers refused to fight him because of his color. At over six feet tall, he was known as the Galveston Giant. For the first few years of his boxing career Jack fought as the all-black heavyweight champion, defeating all his opponents. Most people of the era felt black boxers were inferior. The white boxers refused to fight black boxers in serious matches. To lose to a black boxer would have been career suicide.

Whites and blacks alike loathed his demeanor but admired it as well. Jack ignored the conventional rules of the day. He was brazen in that he dated white women, dressed extravagantly, drove fast cars and lived as he wanted. When taunts came from crowds during his matches he would just smile as if he did not hear them. When other boxers said, he was inferior or "yellow-bellied" he would toy with them in the ring by brutalizing them, instead of just knocking them out as he was capable of doing.

His treatment of his opponents may have been revenge for the many years of mistreatment by the white establishment or, ever the showman, it may have been Jack's way of drawing the audience into the fight. In old movie reels, Jack is seen grabbing his opponents and lifting them up in the air before dropping them to the mat. Jack's success in the ring was driven by his confidence. He knew he could beat any man who dared enter the ring with him. He truly believed it and he lived it. He had an air invincibility about him that permeated his life.

Jack started boxing at 15. He saw a way out of his tough life through boxing. He took on any street matches or underground fights he could get and usually won. He honed his skills and his reputation began to grow. Jack traveled all over the United States taking on more opponents and getting paid much more for each fight. His fighting style was smooth flawless and defensive. He was not a brawler as much as he was a true boxer. Boxing was in its infancy when Jack helped develop techniques that are still used today.

Jack was so confident in his skills he started following the white heavyweight champion, Tommy Burns, around the world taunting him and begging him to give him a title shot. After a promotor in Australia offered Burns a $30,000 purse, Burns finally relented.

The fight took place in Sidney, Australia in 1908. Burns ridiculed Jack saying he was scared and would lose a fight against him because he was black. He slung relentless racial epithets at him. But Jack had gotten what he wanted – an opportunity to fight Burns for the heavyweight championship.

From the moment the bell rang, the fight was over. Jack punished his opponent and mocked Burns and his ringside crew. Though the fight lasted 14 rounds before being stopped, Jack could have knocked him out sooner but chose to toy with Burns.. Jack won the championship and his confidence only grew.

The promotors of the day went on a quest for the "Great White Hope," producing a series of white contenders to take on Jack, but all were defeated. This only lined Jack's pockets and he flaunted his wealth. Jack performed in vaudeville, raced cars, owned a night club, even patented a wrench and experienced life as someone with confidence would, flashing his bright smile.

Jack fought in what was billed the Fight of the Century when he fought Jim Jeffries. Jeffries was lured out of retirement by prize money that had reached over $100,000. Jack beat Jeffries easily, and his defeat sparked white riots across the country. But Jeffries was humbled by and even complimentary of Jack's ability and admitted he could not have beaten him, even in his prime.

Jack's celebrity would be his undoing. He was prosecuted by the government for breaking the Mann Act, a law that made it a felony to engage in interstate transport of any woman for the purpose of prostitution. It was suspect that his case was racially motivated as the "prostitute" was his white girlfriend. It was seen as a way to knock him down a peg, to punish him for his brazenness, success and confidence. Jack lived in exile in France for several years before returning to serve out his term in prison.

Jack was recently pardoned by Donald Trump in 2018 in an effort led by relatives, boxers, and Sylvester Stallone. It took the government over 100 years to recognize it had made a mistake.

Jack was a rare individual whose confidence in his abilities stood out. As a black boxer in the 1900's he had to fight prejudice, hate, and injustice. Jack smiled through it all. His confidence drove his success. He had a true heart of confidence in and out of the ring. Jack lived for himself and he did not care what others thought of him.

I believe once we start to believe in ourselves and our dreams, goals, and aspirations, all will be within our reach. Live life like Jack, smile and be true to yourself.

Questions:

1. In what circumstances, do you feel most confident?
2. Have you ever suffered from a lack of confidence? How did you handle it?
3. What do you think is the best way to promote confidence in your children?

Heart of Humility
William Crawford

"Humility is not thinking less of yourself;
it's thinking of yourself less"
- Rick Warren

I often wave at strangers, people passing by, and I recognize those that are used to not getting noticed. I remember feeling this way. When I was young, I was a special needs student. I had to leave class each day to go the resource room for reading and math. It was embarrassing to me. My family was also poor, so while my clothes may have been clean, they were not new. I wore glasses so kids called me "four eyes." I was shy and did not like to talk to people. I guess I felt inferior.

As I grew, and through hard work achieved some success, I gained confidence and became more outgoing, but I still remember my humble beginnings. I try to befriend people at all rungs of the socioeconomic scale. In restaurants, I will pay the bill for those who are sitting alone.

While waiting in a drive-through at a fast food restaurant, I pay for the person behind me. I like to think I am humble and I do not seek any satisfaction in doing these small things, which pale in comparison to those service men and women who have given their lives, limbs, and souls to serve others. They demonstrate true humility in that they do not seek glory, riches, or fame. They only want to help their team members, unit, and country.

William Crawford could teach us all a lesson in regard to humility. He was awarded the Medal of Honor for his actions in during World War II, but he never sought recognition for the heroism. His heroics took place in a battle near Altavilla, Italy in 1943. Private Crawford was serving as a squad scout. His company's mission was to attack Hill 424, but they came under intense fire and were pinned down. Crawford, with no regard for himself, moved forward under fire and single handedly used grenades and his rifle to take out a machine gun nest. But his unit was still under heavy fire from a second machine gun nest, so Crawford again moved forward and took out the second nest. His company soon took the hill.

Crawford was captured by the enemy while helping an injured soldier. He was presumed dead and his father received his Medal of Honor. When word of this leaked to William's captors, he received better treatment because they respected his heroism. He was a prisoner of war until late in 1944 when he was rescued.

After the war, Crawford married and enlisted back in the army. He spent the next 20 years serving his country. As a Medal of Honor recipient, he was often used in public relations events during his military service. He once got to work on a war movie as a consultant and even attended an event held by President Kennedy at the White House honoring Medal of Honor recipients. While this recognition could have made him egocentric, Crawford always remained humble. He retired from the Army in 1967 as a master sergeant.

He next went to work for the Air Force Academy as a custodian. None of the cadets knew of his heroism and he never mentioned his service. His heart was not one to seek personal glory or acclaim. Crawford took great pride in his work and seemed extremely shy He often went about his daily task of sweeping, mopping, and cleaning the academy unnoticed by cadets as they hurried about. It was not until one of the cadets, who was researching Medal of Honor recipients, discovered his heroic past.

Soon things changed for Crawford. Cadets who normally had not noticed him greeted him offered invitations to events. They asked for his guidance and advice. He happily shared his story with them all, not to bring attention to himself, but to help the cadets grow as young adults and professionals. His demeanor changed and he started walking with a little more pride. He no longer just swept the floors; he mentored these young cadets.

In 1984 Ronald Reagan formally presented Crawford with the Medal of Honor at the Air Force Academy graduation. Ever the humble man, he did his best not to deflect attention away from the cadets during their ceremony. His character of humility and quiet service are to be commended and recognized as an example for all to follow. Live life with a Heart of Humility.

Whenever I focus on my own achievements or am filled with my own self-importance I think of those, like William, who performed amazing acts of service yet never sought recognition. I strive to be more like that.

Questions:

1. Have you ever encountered someone whose background surprised you?
2. In this current "me-focused" social media world, do you think there is a place for humility?
3. Have you ever felt inferior in your own life?

Heart of Honor
Franz Stigler

"No person was ever honored for what he received.
Honor has been the reward for what he gave."
- Calvin Coolidge

My father is my hero. Even in his mid-seventies, if I call him he would be there for me. He loves without judgement and cares deeply for his children. I am humbled by his sacrifices to our family over the years. When we were children, my father would not even touch his food until we had eaten ours because he wanted to make sure there was enough food for us to eat. He was a man of honor who puts our needs first.

Honor among men can take many forms. I believe that there is no honor higher than sparing the life of your enemy.

Franz Stigler demonstrated a heart of honor toward a fellow warrior during WWII. He was a German fighter pilot tasked with taking out B-17 bombers. Stigler was an ace pilot who only needed one more kill to receive the coveted Knight Cross (the highest award in Nazi Germany). But Stigler didn't care about awards nor for putting his kills on his rudder like other pilots. He only did so under orders from his commanders. His upbringing was humble, and he idolized his father who was a gentle and affectionate man. This helped to shape his decision in December 1943.

While flying a mission, Stigler came across a severely damaged B-17 bomber named "Ye Lode Pub." Stigler flew in behind it and was ready for the kill when he noticed the extent of the airplane's damage. He knew that all the crew could not have survived that many bullet and anti-aircraft shells. As he flew in for a closer look, he did not receive any fire from the aircraft.

Stigler then noticed that the engines were sputtering, one stabilizer was completely shot off, and the nose of the craft was open to the elements. He flew up beside the pilots and gestured for them to land. When they refused, he gestured for them to head toward Sweden, which they further refused. Stigler decided he would fly alongside of the craft as it headed back toward England. This was not only a perilous flight for the damaged aircraft but for Stigler himself. He flew with the craft until he knew he was in danger of being shot down. Stigler then saluted the pilots and returned toward Germany.

Not only did Stigler not receive the distinguished Knights Cross, he risked being court martialed for his decision and maybe even put in jail. His personal honor and integrity drove his decision. How often have we given up honor and integrity in our own lives? As a member of a team, have you put yourself before others? Stigler represented true honor in the harshest of environments by allowing the doomed B-17 bomber to fly home to England. He honored his enemy by not taking the lives of those that were defenseless.

Many years after the war, Stigler met one of the men he had spared that cold December day in 1943. That man, Charlie Browne, and Stigler became lifelong friends. When asked about his decision he simply stated, "I didn't have the heart to finish those brave men. I flew beside them for a long time. They were trying desperately to get home, and I was going to let them do that. I could not have shot at them." Is there any truer honor than sparing the life of your enemy?

Questions:

1. What does honor mean to you?
2. Who in your life most displays a heart of honor?
3. What could you do to develop a heart of honor?

CHAPTER 7

BOUNCING BACK FROM ADVERSITY

Heart of Resilience
Anita Hill

"I can be changed by what happens to me.
But I refuse to be reduced by it."
- Maya Angelou

One act changed her life forever. One brave moment to step out of the shadows and allow her voice to be heard. Anita Hill had no desire of becoming the poster child for workforce sexual harassment. She only felt compelled to relay what had happened to her at the hands of a nominee for the highest court in the land. Her testimony to the senate about Clarence Thomas put her in the national spotlight and made her a pariah to many and an inspiration to many more.

Anita came from humble beginnings, growing up on a farm in the small town of Lone Tree, Oklahoma. She was the youngest of 13 children raised in a very religious family. She was extremely smart and a hard worker. Anita graduated as the valedictorian of Morris High School. With a path set for potential greatness, her inner spirit guided her principles. She attended Oklahoma State University and pursued her psychology degree.

She was later accepted and graduated from the prestigious Yale Law School, one of only a few black students in the class. After graduation, she accepted a position with a private law firm in Washington DC. This is where her star would rise and her inner strength would be challenged.

In Washington, she left her law firm to accept a position as legal advisor for Clarence Thomas at the Department of Education's Office of Civil Rights. Anita was in her element, working with civil rights issues. Her new boss seemed to like her and began to feel comfortable enough around Anita to ask her out. But Anita politely turned him down. As their working relationship grew, they probably began cordially discussing personal things with one another. Little did Anita know that Clarence Thomas would soon begin discussing things of a sexual nature when they would have lunch or work late.

Anita would later testify that his discussions became extremely graphic. At the time, she was just beginning her career and Clarence's star was on the rise. She did not say anything for fear of retaliation. Plus, it was the 1980s and women had few rights when it came to sexual harassment.

I would hate for my daughter to feel the way Anita must have felt. If Haley felt dirty or had a pit in her stomach every time she went to work, I would feel like I had failed her. Fortunately, times have changed and women have more recourse today if they are sexually harassed on the job.

As a man approaching 50, to say I have never said anything inappropriate to women would be a lie. After realizing my mistakes, though, I have been much more aware of what I say to others. Words hurt and they are damaging.

For years Anita dealt with constant harassment from Clarence Thomas. Some may wonder why she didn't say anything. But as a woman, and a black woman at that, she didn't feel like she was in a position to do something and eventually the harassment stopped. Yet when Thomas moved to the Equal Opportunity Employment Commission, Anita went with him. However, the sexual harassment soon resumed and this time it was worse. Anita decided it was time to look for another job.

Although her reasons were not known by others, Anita took a stand by leaving the position she held and accepting a professorship at Oral Roberts University. Three years later she became a professor at the University of Oklahoma. Anita's star was on the rise again, and in 1989 she became the first African American tenured professor at the University. Despite the harassment, Anita had remained resilient and just kept moving forward. She was now a tenured professor living back in her home state. She had moved on with her life.

Things soon changed as George H. W. Bush nominated Clarence Thomas in 1991 to succeed Thurgood Marshall on the Supreme Court. Approached by the Senate Judiciary Committee, Hill was reluctant to dredge up the past. She had nothing to gain by coming forward with accusations of sexual harassment.

Knowing the power and influence that a position on the Supreme Court would give Thomas gave her pause and a reason to come forward with the sexual harassment and innuendos she endured. After her statements to the FBI became public, she soon found herself on the senate floor and on national TV answering personal questions about her claims.

Anita became a lightning rod for both sides and the nation. Many of the senators stated she was a scorned woman. Others found the senator's questions to be demeaning and sexist. Anita bravely she sat in front of the senate committee and answered their questions with elegance and grace. She was resilient though. She was there to share her ordeal and did so with honor. Ultimately though, Thomas' nomination was confirmed on Oct. 16, 1991 by the slimmest margin of any judge on the current court.

While her efforts would have appeared to be in vain, Anita's resilience and bravery sparked change. During the 1992 election, many women were empowered to run for office. Five women, including longtime California Senator Diane Feinstein, were elected to the senate that year. Her testimony also brought workplace harassment to the forefront and companies were forced to evaluate and make the necessary changes to prevent such harassment.

Anita turned down many offers to speak about workplace sexual harassment and could have made millions speaking and traveling, but as an intensely private person, she wanted to return to her professorship at the University of Oklahoma. Anita had come forward to share her story because she felt compelled to do so.

However, her Senate testimony did not make her popular at the university, particularly among her conservative colleagues. Internal strife, among other reasons, led her to resign her position. Imagine enduring the public spectacle of the senate hearings to do what you felt was right and then returning to what you thought was a safe place only to be vilified at your job.

Again, Anita was resilient and became a visiting professor at Brandeis University and in 2015 received her full professorship. Anita has written an autobiography and has been depicted in a 2016 movie, Confirmation, about the hearings.

For a long time in the 1980s, Anita remained silent. She chose to move on instead of making waves. When she finally came forward to confront Clarence Thomas she was knocked down. But at every turn Anita demonstrated the true heart of resilience. She left a legacy that has led to less tolerance of sexual harassment and a day of reckoning for some through the #MeToo movement.

If you are willing to get up every time you get knocked down, you have the potential to achieve more and do more than you can ever imagine. Anita is a beautiful example of grace under pressure and the heart of resilience.

There are less well-known examples of such resilience. My stepmother is an amazing lady. Shirley has two boys, one nearing 50 and one just 27 years old. The youngest, Bryant, was born with spastic quadriplegic cerebral palsy. This is the most severe form of cerebral palsy and results in the inability to control and use your legs, arms and body.

Shirley's life immediately changed and she had to stop working to take care of Bryant. Though she was married at the time, her husband was little help. He had nothing to do with his newborn son who he thought would die soon anyway. Imagine a mother having so little support from her husband and having to endure negative comments on a regular basis. What seemed to be a happy marriage before the birth of Bryant, was suddenly thrust into despair.

Shirley was left to care for him every day by herself. While she had help during his first year of life, she mostly cared for him alone. Bryant's father had very little to do with his care, except to provide for the family.

When Bryant was old enough to attend school, Shirley became an advocate for her son and was determined to help other parents with disabled children. If parents were in need, Shirley would find resources to help. But her own life had to be lonely, as she really couldn't talk to her husband about Bryant's needs.

When Bryant turned nine, her husband left. Shirley had no job and no income and soon he stopped paying the bills. Shirley and her son had to survive on Bryant's SSI, which was around $800 a month. Ever resilient, Shirley learned to adjust and to live on this modest income. She took care of Bryant and provided the love and care necessary for his survival.

Due to the severity of Bryant's disability, Shirley lived with the fear of Bryant dying daily. I could not imagine putting my daughter to bed as a small child fearing that she may not wake up the next morning.

Although she is small in stature and he is a grown man, Shirley lifts Bryant up and down with ease. She must change Bryant's diapers, care for him, and do her best to communicate with him with little or no help or assistance from family or friends. She lived in poverty and alone for many years as she struggled to care for Bryant and herself. Shirley is strong in her faith and has relied on prayer. I am amazed at her resilience, perseverance and positive outlook despite all the setbacks she experienced. I can feel her strength and resilience when I talk with her.

Shirley married my father a few years ago and though Bryant lives with them, life is a little easier for both of them now. She brings my dad happiness and clearly he does the same for her when you hear her laugh and see her smile. What I have learned from Shirley and Anita is to handle adversity with grace and perseverance and to get back up every time you get knocked down.

Questions:

1. Did you ever have to take a stand on something that ended up affecting your life in a negative way? What was it?
2. Is there someone you admire for taking a stand?
3. Do you believe you have become more or less resilient as you have grown older?

Heart of Devotion
Hans and Margret Rey

"Being deeply loved by someone gives you strength,
while loving someone deeply gives you courage."
- Lao Tzu

The ties that bind us can be dangerous, tumultuous, adventurous, and bring us closer together than you could ever imagine. Successful marriages are those that can find the humor within their story. The ability to share and laugh about adventures can strengthen the heart and soul of every marriage. Strong couples help each other through the dark days and celebrate the bright days. Each day is an opportunity to grow stronger in your marriage and your devotion to one another.

Some couples manage to weather extraordinary circumstances and emerge stronger for it. That was the case with authors and illustrators Hans and Margret Rey. Their creation, a little fictional monkey, not only saved their lives, but impacted the world.

Hans and Margret Rey were children in Germany when they first met. Hans was artistic and grew up with a love of animals and drawing. Margret also had an affinity for drawing and attended the acclaimed Bauhaus art school. They were also German Jews during Hitler's rise to power in the 1930s.

Hans' family owned a business in Brazil that specialized in housing fixtures. After art school and working in advertising, Margret left Germany for Rio De Janeiro in 1935 to escape Nazism and to find Hans. She challenged him to leave the family business and live his life as he wished. Most people are taught to get an education, a good job and marry. But Margret was encouraging Hans to leave a stable and prosperous career to pursue his artistic dreams.

Hans and Margret would soon marry and go to Paris for their honeymoon. While there, both fell in love with the city and its art, food, and adventures. Before the young couple realized it, they had stayed in Paris for two years, pursuing their talents of drawing and telling stories. Hans and Margret were devoted to one another and to their creations.

The couple started a small advertising agency and began submitting children's stories to publishers. One of these stories was about a Giraffe named Raffy and nine monkeys. One of these young monkeys was Fife, later known as Curious George. The stories were accepted by a British publisher. Life was wonderful for the young couple. They were happy and their careers were beginning to take off.

However, in May of 1940 the Germans invaded France and the Reys were no longer safe living in Paris. Hans and Margret knew they had to leave France if they wanted to survive. They had a little money from their manuscripts, but they were not wealthy. They could not take the trains out of Paris as most had been stopped, and those that did run required identification cards.

They had to devise another plan of escape. Hans contemplated buying a two-person bike so they could take their few belongings and ride out of town, but that required working in unison. While they worked successfully as a team on their children's books, a tandem bike was another matter to Margret. She put her foot down and told Hans to get two bikes. Instead he built two separate bikes from parts he could scrounge together.

Imagine the tension they must have felt trying to escape the place they loved, but had now become too dangerous for them as the German Army approached Paris. Imagine the stress they must have been under, knowing that if they did not escape Paris they could be put to death or sent to a concentration camp.

With bikes built from parts, manuscripts in hand and a few belongings, they rode out of Paris 40 hours before it fell to the Germans. The couple rode their bikes for several days. They slept in barns and in fields before finally making it to the Spanish French border. With passports and identification one would think it might be easy to cross the border, but Hans and Margret were German Jews. The border guard questioned them intensely. Hans explained to the guard they only had some belongings and children's manuscripts.

The guard ask to see the manuscripts. Margaret and Hans began telling the story of Fife and as he read about the adventures of the little French monkey, he began to laugh. Perhaps because the story brightened his day, the guard allowed them to pass through the border. I can only imagine how fearful the Reys were about whether they would be able to pass through and how grateful they were for the antics of their creation, Fife. I like to think that the guard went home that night and entertained his own children by sharing the story of Fife.

With the little money, they had left the couple made their way to Brazil and then onto New York. By the time they got there, they were broke from their travels. Their British publisher came to their aid and helped them get settled. He also encouraged them to change the name of Fife to a more American name, George. Curious George was born.

As Curious George became a household name, Hans and Margret became successful authors and built a wonderful life. From the early 1940s to the mid-1960s, the Reys continued to produce Curious George books, reaching generations of children. I was one of those children. I not only loved reading those stories when I was a child, they helped me learn how to read.

Hans and Margret's story is one of devotion during happy times and under extreme duress. Margret helped Hans to find his calling and fulfill their dreams. They grew closer and comforted one another during stressful times and strengthened their bond.

Angie and Mike have been married for over 30 years. Their marriage is strong and they are devoted to one another. They endured the same struggles that most marriages experience, only they have successfully weathered them. Instead of splitting them apart, their trials and tribulations have brought them closer together. In fact, their struggles helped them get to the enviable place where they are today.

When Angie was in high school she fell in love with Mike and they married and had children at a young age. Mike was making good money, however, in his job at Monsanto, while Angie attended college. For a young, married couple, things seemed to be going well.

Once Angie completed her degree she became an elementary teacher. Mike's career at Monsanto was thriving. Then adversity struck at the least opportune time. Mike was let go from his high-paying job. With a new home, two young boys and bills to pay, the couple were suddenly left to figure out how to make ends meet.

What did Mike and Angie do? They went on a cruise! The tickets were already paid for so they had decided to follow through with it. This one act gave them an opportunity to step back from their situation and plan their next move. While on the cruise, the couple decided to allow Mike to pursue his dreams, even though it meant they would struggle. Mike, a natural caregiver with a passion to help others, was going to college to become a nurse.

With just one income, the bills began to pile up and there were many sleepless nights. But Mike and Angie kept their faith in God and their sense of humor and persevered through the struggles.

Mike graduated from college and became a nurse just in time. The couple's debts had mounted and they were close to losing their home to foreclosure. In a few years, Mike and Angie caught up on their debts and began to live the life they had previously enjoyed and even surpassed it. Angie completed her master's degree and became a school administrator. After many years as a registered nurse, Mike went back to school to become a nurse practitioner.

Today, they both have successful careers. Mike is a nurse practitioner and Angie a principal of a middle school. They have two grown boys. Their family regularly goes on vacations, especially cruises.

A heart of devotion can help you survive life's inevitable ups and downs and overcome adversity. Hans and Margret's devotion to each other and their books helped them escape persecution during World War II and build a new life where they achieved their dreams and influenced others with their stories. Mike and Angie survived a devastating job loss, which resulted in an opportunity to pursue passions which have become thriving and joyful careers. I can happily say that Mike and Angie are back to taking cruises and look back at their challenging times, while painful, as a period of growth that brought them closer together.

Questions:

1. To what or whom are you most devoted?
2. What was a challenging time in your life that brought you and your spouse together?
3. Do you think adversity is required for growth to occur?

Heart of Stoicism
Rubin 'Hurricane" Carter

"No great thing is created suddenly, any more than a bunch of grapes or a fig. If you tell me that you desire a fig; I answer you that there must be time. Let it first blossom, then bear fruit, then ripen."
- Epictetus

Patience is not my strength. When I set my mind to a goal, I can become even more impatient. My poor family must suffer through my OCD and single-mindedness during these periods.

In Desert Storm, I was forced to be patient, because being impatient could lead to a mental breakdown. When my unit first arrived in the desert in January of 1991, we were put in a holding area. These areas were large shipping warehouses along the port. The days were long and miserable, especially for someone like me who lacked patience. We trained to the degree we could considering we had very little equipment. It was on a ship heading our way and until it arrived we were stuck at this port.

We played spades in our spare time, read books, studied and honed our military craft, and did physical fitness training. We practiced military maneuvers on foot, but mostly we waited. I was forced to be patient and to work on my stoicism.

Patient and stoic are not who I am. I must be moving and doing or I get fidgety. But for six months while serving in Desert Storm I was forced to be patient and stoic. Rubin "Hurricane" Carter was forced to be patient and stoic for nearly 20 years while sitting in prison falsely accused of triple murder. If for some unimaginable reason I was sent to prison and was locked up for many years, I don't think I would be able to cope for very long. Rubin endured through stoicism and patience. His was a heart of stoicism.

Rubin "Hurricane" Carter was a prize fighter who was wrongfully convicted of a triple murder in 1966. He was sentenced to prison for 30 years to life. His early life was one of turmoil. His father, a strict disciplinarian, turned him into authorities for stealing clothing from a local department store in New Jersey when he was only nine. Rubin was placed on probation for this incident. He was not a very good student; some would consider him unruly.

Rubin was placed in reform school when he was in the fourth grade. While in the reform school, he stabbed a guard. He claimed self-defense, stating the guard had made sexual advances and tried to throw him off a cliff. After this altercation, Rubin was sent to the Jamesburg State Home for Boys where he experienced extreme physical and mental abuse from the guards. After six years in detention, Rubin escaped and went to live with his aunt who lived in Philadelphia. He enlisted in the army despite still being a fugitive in New Jersey.

Rubin thrived in the army and became a paratrooper for the famous 101St Airborne Division in Germany. It was here that he first put on boxing gloves. He enjoyed training and working with boxers. He considered boxers hard-working, strong, honest, and hard fighters. In this arena, there was no fear. Everything was simple and Rubin excelled. While boxing in the army he won 51 bouts, 35 by knockout, with only 5 losses. Not bad for a man just introduced to the fight game. During his service, he became the army's European light welterweight champion.

Rubin did not just thrive in the ring. He started working on his personal education and took speech therapy to help him overcome his stutter. He became interested in Islamic studies and while he never officially converted, but he would often refer to himself as Saladin Abdullah Muhammad.

Rubin was honorably discharged from the army in 1956. He had gone back to his home in New Jersey and had become a truck driver. But the authorities tracked him down and put him back in prison for his escape from Jamesburg. He would spend the next 10 months at Annandale Reformatory serving out his sentence. Despite the fresh start the army had given him, he was never far from problems with the law.

In 1957, Rubin was released from Annandale but it wasn't long before he was sent to Trenton State Penitentiary for four years for purse snatching and assaulting a man. During his time in prison, Rubin began to live with anger and rage in his heart. He also became interested in boxing again.

Rubin was released from prison in September of 1961 and fought his first professional boxing match for a purse of just $20. As he stated in his autobiography, he was in his element in the ring and he loved it. Promotors loved him because they could sell his image as caged animal let out of prison. One promotor dubbed him Hurricane because of his destructive nature in the ring. He fought well and made a name for himself, beating the welterweight champion in 1963 and, fighting above his weight class, losing a close decision to the middleweight champion.

The police were never far away, though, and Carter flaunted his success with his flamboyant lifestyle and confrontational personality. He even had his name painted on his Cadillac for all to see. The police often harassed Rubin. They would fingerprint him before matches. They would take his picture with the excuse that he was a convicted felon. Rubin was even being monitored by the FBI.

His life would forever change in June of 1966 when he and a friend stayed out late partying and bar hopping in Paterson, New Jersey. During that time, two black men shot and killed three white patrons at a bar. Rubin was not involved in the incident, but the police had it in for him. During the trial, eyewitnesses to the shooting did not identify Rubin as the murderer. Yet two white men with criminal records lied about him and Rubin was sent to prison for 30 years to life.

Rubin was a flamboyant figure who would not have been described as stoic. It was in prison where he was transformed. Rubin refused to wear prison clothes or perform prison jobs as he always maintained his innocence. He refused to eat prison food and sustained himself on canned food. He became an avid reader of law and started studying philosophy, history, religion, and metaphysics. Many times, he was put in solitary confinement for refusing to follow prison rules. He proclaimed, "You may incarcerate my body, but my mind is free."

In the 1970s, Rubin and his wrongful conviction became a cause celebre attracting the attention of many famous people who fought for his release, including Mohammed Ali. Bob Dylan wrote a song, "Hurricane" about his plight.

Despite the renewed attention, Rubin stayed in jail. But he used his time to help fellow inmates with their own trials from the knowledge he had gained reading law books. Rubin developed the heart of a stoic, never displaying his feelings and serving without complaint.

Rubin was released from prison in 1985, when a federal judge overturned his conviction. It took patience for him to be able to fight for his personal freedom for two decades and never give up. It took the heart of a stoic to endure it.

Upon his release, he moved to Canada and became a Canadian citizen. His self-education helped him live the rest of his life happy and free. He founded Innocence International in 2004 and lectured about inequities in America's criminal justice system. He died of cancer in 2014 while still fighting for those wrongfully accused.

He once said that he felt as if his first 49 years on earth were like hell but his last 28 were like living in heaven. At one time in his life he was an angry man who lived hard and flaunted his successes to the police and those within his community. Once he went to prison, he developed a heart of stoicism because he discovered how to control the freedom within.

When I am upset or impatient about work, family, and anything else I cannot control, I take a deep breath and think of Rubin and attempt to control my freedom within.

Questions:

1. 1. How often do we allow outside sources good or bad to control who we are?
2. All of us lose patience with loved ones. What is your most likely trigger?
3. Have you ever had to endure a situation where you were the victim of a misunderstanding or misinformation?

Heart of Ownership
Tony Pollard

"Do your thing. Do it unapologetically. Don't be discouraged by criticism. You probably already know what they're going to say. Pay no mind to the fear of failure. It's far more valuable than success. Take ownership, take chances, and have fun. And no matter what,
don't ever stop doing your thing."
- Asher Roth

Throughout this book, I have discussed extreme cases of adversity and challenges. Each case of doing something from the heart helped those in this book to either find success or to live successfully. Some may not have been rich financially, but they led lives that were rich in achievements and impacting others.

What I have left out was that each person or individual took ownership of their lives. This was my case as well. But it took a major failure before I made a conscious decision to take ownership of my life.

I was the golden boy in my profession. I am an educator by trade. I have taught in inner city schools and lockdown facilities. I have taught upper income students and those who may not have had a nightly dinner or even electricity. These roles helped prepare me to become principal of my own school.

The superintendent called me the Thursday evening after the scheduled board meeting where my new position was officially approved. He said, "Congratulations, Tony! You are going to do a great job." I vowed not to let him down.

Everyone knows I put the students first and that is why I was given this opportunity. My first day was to be June 1, 2013. My daughter was happy and my parents were both extremely proud. I couldn't be more excited. I was ready to take off running. Ideas swirled through my mind and I wrote each one of them down. I was going to turn the school around. I was going to get in the churches, neighborhoods, houses, and whatever else it would take to get the community involved with the school. The teachers were excited about the future. I received so many congratulatory calls from people who knew me personally. I even received calls from those who did not know me very well. It seemed I was destined for this position. I couldn't mess this situation up.

My euphoria would be short lived. I was packing my office up at the school I was leaving. I had spent nights packing the office and days preparing my new office. As you can imagine, I was exhausted. My exhaustion apparently affected my decision-making ability too, which would change me forever.

After spending the entire weekend packing the last of my belongings, I made the ill-fated decision to send out a funny goodbye email to the faculty and staff I adored so much. I pulled up YouTube and started watching videos that would most amuse my faculty. Instead of downloading each video to my desktop, I decided to upload them to my school faculty email list. This is when everything went south.

I watched several videos. Some were appropriate for the workplace and some were not. I thought I would download each one and then watch them again to choose the video that would be the most amusing. In my haste, I deleted all the videos from that e-mail list that I wanted to keep. I left the one video attached to the list that was the most inappropriate. Instead of taking the time to review it one last time, I sent the video out to the faculty and staff I was leaving.

Once I sent the email, I locked up my office and headed home for the night. I would sleep well and head to my new job Monday morning. My dream job awaited me and my experience in dealing with tough parents and students. My dream job needed my ideas and my exuberance.

I arrived at work Monday at around 6:30 am. The superintendent called me around 8 am and nonchalantly said, "Mr. Pollard, you are to report to my office at noon." I assumed it was to sign my contract. The superintendent, who had less than a week earlier called to compliment me, would probably only want to hear my ideas and vision at this point.

I arrived at noon and was directed to the conference room. As I sat waiting for the superintendent, I began planning the remainder of my week at my new job. Within a couple of minutes, in walked the HR director, the superintendent, and the elementary superintendent. My heart skipped a beat; I knew this was bigger than I had originally thought.

The superintendent stated I had sent out an inappropriate video that contained sexually inappropriate material. The video I had sent was 47 seconds long. It was a European commercial that contained fondling between adults.

This was the last thing I thought I might hear coming out of his mouth. I explained that it was just an innocent mistake. I meant to send a different video. The superintendent then said that he could not have someone who was so careless serving as a principal at one of his schools.

I literally thought I was going to lose my lunch. I began to apologize and ask if there was anything I could do to keep my position and put this error in judgment behind me. Tears streamed down my face as I faced these three people. He stated that there was nothing that could be done and I would be placed at another school to serve as an assistant principal. To make matters worse, I wasn't allowed to apologize to those I had offended. I felt awful.

The room was quiet except for me trying to compose myself. What could be done? I had to make a choice quickly. I could fight this and tell them I was getting a lawyer, or I could accept this fate and live to fight another day. In my emotional state, I chose the latter. I would fight another day. I took the blame and admitted that although it was not intentional, I did it, and I accepted my punishment. In my mind, there had to be a way to overcome this, I just could not visualize it in that moment. I was losing everything. My stellar reputation was now in the garbage, essentially because of a 47-second video that I mistakenly published in an attempt to leave a lighthearted farewell to my colleagues.

I left the conference room and headed home. On my way, I pulled into a large parking lot near a Sam's Club. I immediately made a post on Facebook that I had ruined my life. I had embarrassed my daughter, my wife, and ruined my career. This post was obviously made in the heat of the moment and perhaps foolish. I am glad I made the post, though because once I saw it on my Facebook page I realized I was letting the situation defeat me. I realized that the post was weak. Within two hours of making the post, I deleted it.

This fight (life event) changed me completely. I took control of my CRD (courage, resilience, and discipline). I made a conscious decision to demonstrate to my daughter, wife, friends, and family, that I could bounce back after a knockout. The first step was to live with a heart of ownership.

It was failure and my ownership of that failure that led me to begin speaking and writing. I have a long way to go to achieve my ultimate goals. I also know that had I not decided to own my mistake that I would not be working to achieve those goals.

I share that story, which some may think would be embarrassing, for a reason. There are moments that define our lives. This was my moment. I have experienced both war and divorce, which had a profound effect on me. Losing my job for the reasons I did was public and perhaps shameful. When I decided to take ownership, I said to the world watch out here I come. I also said to my daughter that no matter how bad it gets and it will get bad you must get back up.

Everyone in this story took ownership of their lives. Everyone decided to live fully and many changed the lives of their, family, community, and even their country all because they took extreme ownership of their own lives. Live with a heart of ownership.

Questions:

1. Have you ever been humbled because of a mistake? What was it?
2. Do you believe you have taken ownership of your life?
3. Do you think ownership and responsibility are one and the same?

FROM THE HEART EPILOGUE

The from the heart journey all started with a speech I gave to a group of about 30 veterans at Baldwin County Electric Cooperative. The speech was titled courage, resilience, and discipline. I gave everyone in the group a small heart I had purchased from the Build-a-Bear store.

Several of the veterans came up after the fifteen-minute speech and thanked me and one even shared his story about his time in Afghanistan and Iraq. I was touched by his story and realized I had something to share. I started sharing my own experiences from war, life, and work, and before I knew it I was giving out hearts after every speech I gave.

I now have a goal of putting a heart in hands of everyone in the world. I have had teachers show me their hearts that they keep on themselves. I explained that when you are having a bad day just pull out the heart and think of someone from one of the stories I have shared who had much more than just a bad day. Then smile and put the heart back in your pocket.

Students I have spoken to have given their hearts to those they have a crush on. Others have shared these stories with their parents. The little heart started as a simple gesture on my part to remind the listener of the story that was shared.

This book has helped me realize that I can overcome all my weaknesses. I can set big goals and although I am nearly 50, I can still achieve those goals. I realize now more than ever that I spent a lot of time living in fear of failure and that I wasted a lot of years not living my dreams and goals to the fullest. Since this realization, I have now run two marathons. I have participated in overnight ruck marches. I have run obstacle course races. I am living my dreams.

My daughter Haley, who was floundering in one of my stories, is now doing well. Haley has finally found her joy as an avionics technician and is doing something she really enjoys. As soon as she was hired, she called me, ecstatic. Her voice even reflected someone who seemed more mature and confident.

My wife Terri, who struggles with her own demons, has found her passion in teaching fitness classes. Terri is in her 50s, but when she turned 50 we started going backwards with her age, so we say she is in her mid-40s. She not only looks beautiful, she is beautiful. I am extremely proud of her. As she got older and began experiencing life changes, she seemed to have lost her joy. For a couple of years Terri really struggled but now she is excited and nervous each time she teaches a new fitness class.

She has found her joy and it is so evident in how she greets me and the world every day. Terri is living from the heart and I love it for her and for me as well. Haley is living from the heart in the joy she has found in her new career, which make me worry a little less.

My goal is to not only put a heart in the hands of everyone in the world, I want to help businesses and employees realize we can be better. We can perform at a higher level in all our endeavors and approach our jobs, businesses, employees, and customers with a desire to make them better and to make ourselves better as individuals.

I want teachers, educators, and those who work in public service to not allow the monthly guaranteed check to make them complacent. I hope to see them continue living with passion. These incredible professionals started down this path because they had a goal to add value to the world and to provide service from the heart with zeal and without apprehension.

I want to see them keep that fire burning or to help them rekindle the fire they may have lost. We should strive to be "ALL IN" in all we do. To be "ALL IN", we must do things from the heart.

This book is about me, my family, friends and of course, some special people, both well-known and lesser-known. It is about overcoming and growing from adversity to create, help, or make us better as human beings. The research is clear, 75% of the world deals with adversity of some kind. It is how you handle it that makes the difference. Those who fight through it add something special to the world around them.

When I look at photos of me as a young father holding and beholding my baby in my arms, you can tell it was heaven for me. I was living completely without fear from the heart. Haley was my world and I could not imagine not being there for her. That little baby had my heart from the moment she was born.

That love I felt is how all of us should live our lives. Completely without fear or compromise, all from the heart.

INDEX

REFERENCES:

- 4 Secrets of the Tarahumara That Will Improve Your Running | Competitor.com. (2016). Competitor.com. Retrieved 6 July 2018, from http://running.competitor.com/2016/02/training/four-running-secrets-of-the-tarahumara_145377

- About World War 2: A Small Christmas Truce. (2018). Owlcation. Retrieved 1 September 2018, from https://owlcation.com/humanities/About-World-War-2-A-Small-Christmas-Truce

- Amelia Earhart Biography: A Record Setting Pilot. (2018). YouTube. Retrieved 26 July 2018, from https://www.youtube.com/watch?v=tjTSMMnxDZk

- Amelia Earhart. (2018). Biography. Retrieved 22 July 2018, from https://www.biography.com/people/amelia-earhart-9283280

- Amelia Earhart. (2018). En.wikipedia.org. Retrieved 22 July 2018, from https://en.wikipedia.org/wiki/Amelia_Earhart

- Amelia Earhart. (2018). YouTube. Retrieved 26 July 2018, from https://www.youtube.com/watch?v=EbY2LxFskdI

- American Masters billie jean king. (2019). YouTube. Retrieved 30 September 2019, from https://www.youtube.com/watch?v=ic4bIPVOzXE

- Anita Hill | Biography & Facts. (2020). Encyclopedia Britannica. Retrieved 28 January 2020, from https://www.britannica.com/biography/Anita-Hill

- Anita Hill Reimagining Equality: Stories of Gender, Race, and Finding Home **(2011).**

- Barbara C. Jordan. (2020). HISTORY. Retrieved 9 April 2020, from https://www.history.com/topics/black-history/barbara-c-jordan

- Barbara Jordan. (2020). Biography. Retrieved 9 April 2020, from https://www.biography.com/law-figure/barbara-jordan

- Barbara Jordan. (2020). En.wikipedia.org. Retrieved 9 April 2020, from https://en.wikipedia.org/wiki/Barbara_Jo

- Bertoni, S. (2020). Chuck Feeney: The Billionaire Who Is Trying To Go Broke. Forbes. Retrieved 14 April 2020, from https://www.forbes.com/sites/stevenbertoni/2012/09/18/chuck-feeney-the-billionaire-who-is-trying-to-go-broke/#67f565cb291c

- Bill Crawford, Ten Lessons from a Janitor. (2018). Homeofheroes.com. Retrieved 9 July 2018, from http://www.homeofheroes.com/profiles/profiles_crawford_10lessons.html

- Billie Jean King Accomplishments | Billie Jean King. (2019). Billie Jean King Enterprises. Retrieved 30 September 2019, from https://www.billiejeanking.com/biography/

- Billie Jean King Biography - family, children, parents, mother, old, information, born, husband, year. (2019). Notablebiographies.com. Retrieved 6 October 2019, from https://www.notablebiographies.com/Jo-Ki/King-Billie-Jean.html

- Biography for Master Sergeant Woodrow Keeble Winner of Medal of Honor for the United States Army. (2018). Army.mil. Retrieved 5 July 2018, from https://www.army.mil/medalofhonor/keeble/profile/index.html

- Burlock, M. (2014). The "Fastest Bicycle Rider in the World:" Marshall Walter "Major" Taylor (1878-1932). Hoosier State Chronicles: Indiana's Digital Newspaper Program. Retrieved 5 July 2018, from https://blog.newspapers.library.in.gov/the-fastest-bicycle-rider-in-the-world-marshall-walter-major-taylor-1878-1932/

- Buster Douglas GamesCricketRugbyCFL, &., Softball, N., Sports, O., FB, R., BB, R., Olympics, S. and Games, X.

- Calcara, T., Boxing, R., Boxing, R., Nieves, P., Boxing, R., & Diaz, J. et al. (2018). Fight Night Flashback | Mike Tyson vs. Buster Douglas. Roundbyroundboxing.com. Retrieved 20 July 2018, from https://roundbyroundboxing.com/fight-night-flashback-mike-tyson-vs-buster-douglas/

- Calvin Graham Heart of a childThe Boy Who Became a World War II Veteran at 13 Years Old. Smithsonian. Retrieved 20 July 2018, from https://www.smithsonianmag.com/history/the-boy-who-became-a-world-war-ii-veteran-at-13-years-old-168104583/

- Calvin Graham, 12 Year Old Sailor in WWII. (2016). A War to be Won. Retrieved 20 July 2018, from http://ww2awartobewon.com/wwii-articles/calvin-graham-12-year-old-sailor-wwii/

- Calvin L. Graham: America's Youngest WWII Hero. WAR HISTORY ONLINE. Retrieved 20 July 2018, from https://www.warhistoryonline.com/instant-articles/calvin-l-graham-americas-youngest-wwii-hero.html

- Carter, R. (2018). Rubin Carter. Biography. Retrieved 21 July 2018, from https://www.biography.com/people/rubin-carter-9542248

- Changing the Face of Medicine | Mary Edwards Walker. (2019). Cfmedicine.nlm.nih.gov. Retrieved 7 June 2019, from https://cfmedicine.nlm.nih.gov/physicians/biography_325.html

- Christmas Truce: About World War 2: A Small Christmas Truce

- Chuck Feeney. (2020). En.wikipedia.org. Retrieved 14 April 2020, from https://en.wikipedia.org/wiki/Chuck_Feen

- Chuck Feeney's Story – Intro. (2020). The Atlantic Philanthropies. Retrieved 14 April 2020, from https://www.atlanticphilanthropies.org/chuck-feeneys-story

- Curious About George? Houghtonmifflinbooks.com. Retrieved 21 January 2020, from http://www.houghtonmifflinbooks.com/feat

- Daily Life in the Warsaw Ghetto. (2020). Imperial War Museums. Retrieved 24 February 2020, from https://www.iwm.org.uk/history/daily-life-in-the-warsaw-ghetto

- Daniel Hale Williams. (2020). Biography. Retrieved 9 April 2020, from https://www.biography.com/scientist/daniel-hale-williams

- Daniel Hale Williams. (2020). En.wikipedia.org. Retrieved 9 April 2020, from https://en.wikipedia.org/wiki/Daniel_Hale

- Dashrath Manjhi Road. (2018). Atlas Obscura. Retrieved 25 August 2018, from https://www.atlasobscura.com/places/dashrath-manjhi-road

- Dashrath Manjhi: Some lesser known facts on the Mountain Man who worked for 22 years and carved a path through a mountain. (2018). India Today. Retrieved 19 August 2018, from https://www.indiatoday.in/education-today/gk-current-affairs/story/dashrath-manjhi-282520-2015-07-15Website

- Dashrath Manjhi." En.wikipedia.org. N. p., 2018. Web. 25 Aug. 2018.

- Demosthenes - Crystalinks. (2019). Crystalinks.com. Retrieved 29 September 2019, from https://www.crystalinks.com/demosthenes.html https://cfmedicine.nlm.nih.gov/physicians/biography_325.html

- Demosthenes - Livius. (2019). Livius.org. Retrieved 29 September 2019, from https://www.livius.org/articles/person/demosthenes-politician/

- Demosthenes | Greek statesman and orator. (2018). Encyclopedia Britannica. Retrieved 12 September 2018, from https://www.britannica.com/biography/Demosthenes-Greek-statesman-and-orator

- Doug Criss, C. (2018). He donated blood every week for 60 years and saved the lives of 2.4 million babies. CNN. Retrieved 21 July 2018, from https://www.cnn.com/2018/05/11/health/james-harrison-blood-donor-retires-trnd/index.html

- Dr. Daniel Hale Williams? | Jackson Heart Study Graduate Training and Education Center. (2020). Jsums.edu. Retrieved 9 April 2020, from http://www.jsums.edu/gtec/dr-daniel-hale-william

- Dwight D. Eisenhower | Cold War, Presidency, & Facts. (2020). Encyclopedia Britannica. Retrieved 18 April 2020, from https://www.britannica.com/biography/Dwight-D-Eisenhower

- Dwight D. Eisenhower | The White House. (2020). The White House. Retrieved 18 April 2020, from https://www.whitehouse.gov/about-the-white-house/presidents/dwight-d-eisenhower/

- Dwight D. Eisenhower. (2020). Biography. Retrieved 18 April 2020, from https://www.biography.com/us-president/dwight-d-eisenhower

- Dwight D. Eisenhower. (2020). En.wikipedia.org. Retrieved 18 April 2020, from https://en.wikipedia.org/wiki/Dwight

- Earhart?, W. (2018). Amelia Earhart - Facts & Summary - HISTORY. com. HISTORY.com. Retrieved 23 July 2018, from https://www.history. com/topics/amelia-earhart

- Edwards, J. (2016). When Cadets At The US Air Force Academy Realized Their Janitor Was Medal Of Honor War Hero. WAR HISTORY ONLINE. Retrieved 9 July 2018, from https://www.warhistoryonline. com/world-war-ii/air-force-academy-janitor-medal-of_honor-x.html

- Field, S. (2020). Hedy Lamarr: The Incredible Mind Behind Secure WiFi, GPS And Bluetooth. Forbes. Retrieved 9 April 2020, from https://www. forbes.com/sites/shivaunefield/2018/02/28/hedy-lamarr-the-incredible-mind-behind-secure-wi-fi-gps-bluetooth/#34a164541b79

- GamesCricketRugbyCFL, &., Softball, N., Sports, O., FB, R., BB, R., Olympics, S., & Games, X. (2018). The day James "Buster" Douglas shook the world. ESPN.com. Retrieved 20 July 2018, from http://www. espn.com/boxing/story/_/page/blackhistoryBOX1/the-day-james-buster-douglas-shook-world

- George Foreman - "Monster". (2018). YouTube. Retrieved 7 July 2018, from https://www.youtube.com/watch?v=PiMLt2oSRaQ

- George Foreman | Biography & Record. (2018). Encyclopedia Britannica. Retrieved 7 July 2018, from https://www.britannica.com/biography/George-Foreman

- George Foreman. (2018). Biography. Retrieved 7 July 2018, from https://www.biography.com/people/george-foreman-92988

- George Foreman. (2018). En.wikipedia.org. Retrieved 7 July 2018, from https://en.wikipedia.org/wiki/George_Fore

- Greta Thunberg - Inspiring Others to Take a Stand Against Climate Change | The Daily Show. (2020). YouTube. Retrieved 24 January 2020, from https://www.youtube.com/watch?v=rhQVustYV24

- Greta Thunberg on Whether She'd Meet with the President. (2020). YouTube. Retrieved 24 January 2020, from https://www.youtube. com/watch?v=rsNskDfd5CM

- Greta Thunberg to world leaders: 'How dare you? You have stolen my dreams and my childhood'. (2020). YouTube. Retrieved 24 January2020, from https://www.youtube.com/watch?v=TMrtLsQbaok

- Greta Thunberg. (2020). Biography. Retrieved 24 January 2020, from https://www.biography.com/activist/greta-thunberg

- Hachiko Real Story. (2018). YouTube. Retrieved 8 July 2018, from https://www.youtube.com/watch?v=fJxgu8TtIWI

- Hachikō. (2018). En.wikipedia.org. Retrieved 8 July 2018, from https://en.wikipedia.org/wiki/Hachik%C5%8D

- Hammond, T. (2018). William H. Carney: The first black soldier to earn the Medal of Honor. Military Times. Retrieved 18 April 2020, from https://www.militarytimes.com/military-honor/black-military-

- Hazen Pingree, | Detroit Historical Society. (2020). Detroithistorical. org. Retrieved 1 April 2020, from https://detroithistorical.org/learn/encyclopedia-of-detroit/pingree-hazen

- Hazen Pingree: Quite possibly Detroit's finest mayor. (2020). detroitnews. Retrieved 1 April 2020, from https://www.detroitnews.com/story/news/local/michigan-history/2020/02/08/hazen-pingree-quite-possibly-detroits-finest-mayor/4686854002/

- Hazen S. Pingree Monument | Historic Detroit. (2020). Historicdetroit. org. Retrieved 3 April 2020, from https://historicdetroit.org/buildings/hazen-s-pingree-monument

- Hedy Lamarr. (2020). Biography. Retrieved 9 April 2020, from https://www.biography.com/actor/hedy-lamarr

- Hedy Lamarr. (2020). En.wikipedia.org. Retrieved 9 April 2020, from https://en.wikipedia.org/wiki/Hedy_Lama

- History from WWII - The Charlie Brown and Franz Stigler Incident - Globalo. (2017). Globalo. Retrieved 6 July 2018, from http://www.globalo.com/history-wwii-charlie-brown-franz-stigler-incident/

- History, U. (2019). Dr. Mary Edwards Walker | Center of Military History. History.army.mil. Retrieved 7 June 2019, from https://history.army.mil/news/2016/160200a_maryEdwardsWalker.html

- How Curious George Escaped from Nazis. (2016). The Daily Beast. Retrieved 21 January 2020, from https://www.thedailybeast.com/how-curious-george-escaped-from-nazis?ref=scroll

- If God wills it: St. Therese's Audience with the Pope. (2016). National Shrine and Museum of St. Therese. Retrieved 28 September 2019, from https://saint-therese.org/life-of-st-therese/god-wills-st-thereses-audience-pope/

- Irena Sendler - Rescuer of the Children of Warsaw. (2020). Chabad. org. Retrieved 24 February 2020, from https://www.chabad.org/theJewishWoman/article_cdo/aid/939081/jewish/Irena-Sendler.htm

- Irena Sendler, Warsaw. (2020). Encyclopedia.ushmm.org. Retrieved 24 February 2020, from https://encyclopedia.ushmm.org/contentIrena Sendler. (2020). En.wikipedia.org. Retrieved 24 February 2020, from https://en.wikipedia.org/wiki/Irena_Sendle

- Irena Sendler, Yadvashem.org. Retrieved 24 February 2020, from https://www.yadvashem.org/yv/en/exhibitions/righteous-women/sendler.asp

- Jack Johnson (boxer). (2018). En.wikipedia.org. Retrieved 9 July 2018, from https://en.wikipedia.org/wiki/Jack_Johnson_(boxer)

- Jack Johnson (PBS). (2018). YouTube. Retrieved 9 July 2018, from https://www.youtube.com/watch?v=uK4uBFe7waw

- James Harrison (blood donor). (2018). En.wikipedia.org. Retrieved 21 July 2018, from https://en.wikipedia.org/wiki/James_Harrison_(blood_donor)

- Janusz korczak - Google Search. (2020). Google.com. Retrieved 25 February 2020, from https://www.google.com search?q=janusz+korczak&rlz=1C5CHFS733US734&oq=janusz+ko&aqs=chrome.0.0l2j69i57j0l5.7132j0j8&sourceid =chrome&ie=UTF-8

- Janusz Korczak | www.yadvashem.org. (2020). Yadvashem.org. Retrieved 25 February 2020, from https://www.yadvashem.org/education/educational-materials/learning-environment/janusz-korczak/korczak-bio.html

- Janusz Korczak. (2017). En.wikipedia.org. Retrieved 25 February 2020, from https://en.wikipedia.org/wiki/Janusz_Korc

- Janusz Korczak. (2020). Culture.pl. Retrieved 25 February 2020, from https://culture.pl/en/article/12-things-worth-knowing-about-janusz-korczak

- John Blake, C. (2018). Two enemies discover a 'higher call' in battle - CNN. CNN. Retrieved 6 July 2018, from https://www.cnn.com/2013/03/09/living/higher-call-military-chivalry/index.html

- Johnson, J. (2018). Jack Johnson. Biography. Retrieved 9 July 2018, from https://www.biography.com/people/jack-johnson-9355980

- Kris Carr, New York Times best-selling author and wellness activist. (2020). KrisCarr.com. Retrieved 9 April 2020, from https://kriscarr.com/

- Kris Carr. (2015). En.wikipedia.org. Retrieved 9 April 2020, from https://en.wikipedia.org/wiki/Kris_Carr

- Madam C.J. Walker | African-American Entrepreneur, Philanthropist, and Activist. (2020). Madamcjwalker.com. Retrieved 8 April 2020, from http://madamcjwalker.com/

- Madam C.J. Walker. (2020). Biography. Retrieved 8 April 2020, from https://www.biography.com/inventor/madam-cj-walker

- Madam C.J. Walker's Hair-Care Empire?. Vanity Fair. Retrieved 8 April 2020, from https://www.vanityfair.com/hollywood/2020/03/self-made-madam-cj-walker-company

- Marshall "Major" Taylor: The incredible story of the first African-American world champion. (2014). National Museum of American History. Retrieved 5 July 2018, from http://americanhistory.si.edu/blog/2014/03/marshall-major-taylor-the-incredible-story-of-the-first-african-american-world-champion.html

- Marshall Taylor. (2018). En.wikipedia.org. Retrieved 21 July 2018, from https://en.wikipedia.org/wiki/Marshall_Taylor

- Marshall Taylor. (2018). En.wikipedia.org. Retrieved 5 July 2018, from https://en.wikipedia.org/wiki/Marshall_Taylor

- Mary Walker. (2019). Biography. Retrieved 7 June 2019, from https://www.biography.com/activist/mary-walker

- Mclaughlin, W. (2014). MUST READ: The story behind Charlie Brown & Franz Stigler incident. WAR HISTORY ONLINE. Retrieved 6 July 2018, from https://www.warhistoryonline.com/war-articles/64443.html

- Meet Sgt. William Carney: The first African-American Medal of Honor recipient. (2020). www.army.mil. Retrieved 18 April 2020, from https://www.army.mil/article/181896

- Mike Tyson vs. Buster Douglas. (2018). En.wikipedia.org. Retrieved 20 July 2018, from https://en.wikipedia.org/wiki/Mike_Tyson_vs._Buster_Douglas

- New G.M. Chief Is Company Woman, Born to It. (2020). Nytimes.com. Retrieved 15 January 2020, from https://www.nytimes.com/2013/12/11/business/gm-names-first-female-chief-executive.html

- news, C. (2017). Christmas Eve miracle brought German & American soldiers together | God Reports. Blog.godreports.com. Retrieved 24 July 2018, from http://blog.godreports.com/2017/12/wwii-christmas-eve-miracle-brought-german-american-soldiers-together/ (2018). Ba-ez.org. Retrieved 24 July 2018, from http://ba-ez.org/educatn/lc/oralhist/vincken.htm

- news, C. (2017). Christmas Eve miracle brought German & American soldiers together | God Reports. Blog.godreports.com. Retrieved 1 September 2018, from https://blog.godreports.com/2017/12/wwii-christmas-eve-miracle-brought-german-american-soldiers-together/

- News, M. (2011). Story told of Medal of Honor recipient who lived modest life as janitor. Medal of Honor News. Retrieved 9 July 2018, from https://medalofhonornews.com/2011/05/story-told-of-medal-of-honor-recipient.html

- Oberleutnant Ludwig Franz Stigler. (2018). Warthunder.com. Retrieved 6 July 2018, from https://warthunder.com/en/news/2771--en

- Patrick, B. (2020). Sgt. William H. Carney. Military.com. Retrieved 18 April 2020, from https://www.military.com/history/sgt-william-h-carney.html

- R. G. LeTourneau. (2020). En.wikipedia.org. Retrieved 6 February 2020, from https://en.wikipedia.org/wiki/R._G._LeTo

- R.G. LeTourneau and How God Shaped His Life Through Work | Center for Faith & Work at LeTourneau University. (2018). Centerforfaithandwork.com. Retrieved 6 February 2020, from https://centerforfaithandwork.com/article/surprising-things-you-may-not-know-about-rg-letourneau-and-how-god-shaped-his-life-through

- Raab, S. (2016). Rubin (Hurricane) Carter, Boxer Found Wrongly Convicted, Dies at 76. Nytimes.com. Retrieved 22 July 2018, from https://www.nytimes.com/2014/04/21/sports/rubin-hurricane-carter-fearsome-boxer-dies-at-76.html

- Rarámuri. (2018). En.wikipedia.org. Retrieved 6 July 2018, from https://en.wikipedia.org/wiki/Rar%C3%A1muri

- Rare Jack Johnson Documentary. (2018). YouTube. Retrieved 9 July 2018, from https://www.youtube.com/watch?v=IWHpEUelQzs

- Research, C. (2020). Mary Barra Fast Facts. CNN. Retrieved 15 January 2020, from https://www.cnn.com/2014/04/01/us/mary-barra-fast-facts/index.html

- Reys YouTube. (2020). Youtube.com. Retrieved 21 January 2020, from https://www.youtube.com/watch?v=hm09dAsynAs

- RG LeTourneau – Christian Businessman & Inventor. (2020). Giantsforgod.com. Retrieved 6 February 2020, from http://www.giantsforgod.com/rg-letourneau/

- RG LeTourneau The Curious Life & Career of R.G. LeTourneau. TheBestSchools.org. Retrieved 3 February 2020, from https://thebestschools.org/magazine/rg-letourneau/

- Saint Therese, "The Little Flower" | Society of the Little Flower - US. (2019). Society of the Little Flower - US. Retrieved 28 September 2019, from https://www.littleflower.org/therese/

- Sandomir, R. (2018). AT DINNER WITH: George Foreman; Round Two. Nytimes.com. Retrieved 7 July 2018, from https://www.nytimes.com/1995/05/24/garden/at-dinner-with-george-foreman-round-two.html

- Shania Twain on abuse, betrayal and finding her voice: 'I wanted a break – but not for 15 years'. the Guardian. Retrieved 12 February 2020, from https://www.theguardian.com/music/2018/apr/22/shania-twain-unexpected-return-freak-illness-country-pop-star

- Shania Twain Opens Up About Brutal Abuse By Stepfather. (2020). Country Rebel. Retrieved 16 February 2020, from https://countryrebel.com/blogs/videos/shania-twain-reveals-brutal-abuse-that-nearly-prevented-her-from-singing/

- Shania Twain. (2020). Biography. Retrieved 12 February 2020, from https://www.biography.com/musician/shania-twain

- Shania Twain. (2020). En.wikipedia.org. Retrieved 12 February 2020, from https://en.wikipedia.org/wiki/Shania_T

- Singh, A. (2009). St Therese of Lisieux: who was she?. Telegraph.co.uk. Retrieved 28 September 2019, from https://www.telegraph.co.uk/news/uknews/6198291/St-Therese-of-Lisieux-who-was-she.html

- Steve Irwin | Biography, Death, & Facts. (2020). Encyclopedia Britannica. Retrieved 3 April 2020, from https://www.britannica.com/biography/Steve-Irwin

- Steve Irwin: The incredible story of the wildlife warrior. (2006). The Independent. Retrieved 3 April 2020, from https://www.independent.co.uk/news/people/profiles/steve-irwin-the-incredible-story-of-the-wildlife-warrior-414731.html

- Steve Irwin. (2020). En.wikipedia.org. Retrieved 3 April 2020, from https://en.wikipedia.org/wiki/Steve_Irwin

- Sybil Ludington | American Revolutionary War heroine. (2020). Encyclopedia Britannica. Retrieved 6 April 2020, from https://www.britannica.com/biography/

- Sybil Ludington. (2020). En.wikipedia.org. Retrieved 6 April 2020, from https://en.wikipedia.org/wiki/Sybil_Ludi

- Sybil Ludington. (2020). National Women's History Museum. Retrieved 6 April 2020, from https://www.womenshistory.org/education-resources/biographies/sybil-ludington

- Tarahumara | people. (2018). Encyclopedia Britannica. Retrieved 6 July 2018, from https://www.britannica.com/topic/Tarahu

- Taylor, M. (2018). Major Taylor. Biography. Retrieved 21 July 2018, from https://www.biography.com/people/marshall-walter-major-taylorYou are being redirected.... (2018). Maricopa-az.gov. Retrieved 21 July 2018, from http://www.maricopa-az.gov/web/featured-contributors/2002-marshall-walter-major-taylor-1878-1932-world-record-cyclist

- Taylor, M. (2018). Major Taylor. Biography. Retrieved 5 July 2018, from https://www.biography.com/people/marshall-walter-major-taylor

- The Amazing And True Story Of Hachiko The Dog. (2014). Nerd Nomads. Retrieved 8 July 2018, from https://nerdnomads.com/hachiko_the_dog

- The broke billionaire - Chuck Feeney . (2020). IrishCentral.com. Retrieved 14 April 2020, from https://www.irishcentral.com/opinion/niallodowd/broke-billionaire-chuck-feeney

- The Official Website of Billie Jean King. (2019). Billie Jean King Enterprises. Retrieved 30 September 2019, from https://www.billiejeanking.com/

- The Official Website of Billie Jean King. (2019). Billie Jean King Enterprises. Retrieved 6 October 2019, from https://www.billiejeanking.com/

- The real reason Amelia Earhart is so famous. (2018). YouTube. Retrieved 26 July 2018, from https://www.youtube.com/watch?v=XspEs1x9cPU

- Unforgivable Blackness . Jack Johnson: Rebel of the Progressive Era | PBS. (2018). Pbs.org. Retrieved 9 July 2018, from https://www.pbs.org/unforgivableblackness/rebel/

- Valentina Tereshkova | Biography, Vostok 6, & Facts. (2020). Encyclopedia Britannica. Retrieved 6 April 2020, from https://www.britannica.com/biography/Valentina-Tereshkova

- Valentina Tereshkova: First Woman in Space. Space.com. Retrieved 6 April 2020, from https://www.space.com/21571-valentina-tereshkova.html

- Valentina Tereshkova. (2020). Biography. Retrieved 6 April 2020, from https://www.biography.com/astronaut/valentina-tereshkova

- Valentina Tereshkova. (2020). En.wikipedia.org. Retrieved 6 April 2020, from https://en.wikipedia.org/wiki/Valentina

- Vilchis, R. (2015). Still, They Endure: The Paradox of Mexico's Legendary Tarahumara Runners. Remezcla. Retrieved 6 July 2018, from http://remezcla.com/features/sports/tarahumara-born-to-run-mexico/

- William Harvey Carney. (2020). En.wikipedia.org. Retrieved 18 April 2020, from https://en.wikipedia.org/wiki/William_Ha

- William J. Crawford. (2018). En.wikipedia.org. Retrieved 9 July 2018, from https://en.wikipedia.org/wiki/William_J._Crawford

- Winner of Medal of Honor for the United States Army. (2018). Army.mil. Retrieved 5 July 2018, from https://www.army.mil/medalofhonor/keeble/citation/president.html

- Woodrow Keeble - Recipient - Military Times Hall of Valor. (2018). Valor.militarytimes.com. Retrieved 5 July 2018, from https://valor.militarytimes.com/hero/3410

- Woodrow W. "Woody" Keeble: An American Hero. (2008). Military History. Retrieved 5 July 2018, from https://militaryhistoryblog.wordpress.com/2008/03/08/woodrow-w-woody-keeble-an-american-hero/

- Woodrow W. Keeble - Native Americans in the United States Army. (2018). Army.mil. Retrieved 5 July 2018, from https://www.army.mil/americanindians

- Woodrow W. Keeble. (2018). En.wikipedia.org. Retrieved 5 July 2018, from https://en.wikipedia.org/wiki/Woodrow_W._Keeble

- Woody Keeble proved his mettle long before earning the Medal. (2018). National Guard. Retrieved 5 July 2018, from http://www.nationalguard.mil/News/Article/573194/woody-keeble-proved-his-mettle-long-before-earning-the-medal/